Whiskey Lore's Travel Guide To

EXPERIENCING KENTUCKY BOURBON

Learn • Plan • Taste • Tour

by

Drew Hannush

ISBN: 978-1-7348651-0-3
Kindle ISBN: 978-1-7348651-1-0

DEDICATION

*To my mother Barbara who helped me find a deeper
understanding of myself and the world around me.*

*To my father Russell, who gave me the gift of
wanderlust and a deep love of history.*

Table of Contents

Introduction

MY ROUNDABOUT WAY TO BOURBON

Looking back, my journey to bourbon got off to a very rocky start. It is a story as old as humanity. Wanting to prove that I was a man, and that I could handle my alcohol, as a teenager I overindulged with a bottle of Tennessee sour mash whiskey. Without going into graphic detail, I saw a lot of the porcelain god that evening.

I couldn't shake the experience. For the next 20 years I did everything I could to avoid brown liquor. Just the smell of whiskey was enough to set off my gag reflex.

Lesson learned—the hard way.

That was how beer initially became my drink of choice. While at college in Pennsylvania, I could head to the beer warehouse and buy a case of Schlitz *(I know, I know)* for just $5.99. After college I stepped up my game by turning to more flavorful and substantial imports; in fact, I would have kept my attention entirely outside the US borders if it hadn't been for bumping into Samuel Adams and the craft-beer revolution.

Beer was low-hanging fruit: I could find it everywhere, there were lots of varieties, and a plethora of brands to choose from. Plus, there wasn't a lot of mystery to it. Just look at the package and you would know that it was cherry wheat, chocolate stout, or raspberry lambic. The only drawbacks were the stuffy noses it gave me and the bloating. But these were sacrifices I was willing to make.

Then one day I rented the movie *Sideways* starring Paul Giamatti and Thomas Haden Church. In it, a wine connoisseur takes his soon-to-be married friend on a trip to Napa Valley—California's wine country. What is so quirky and funny about this movie is how, despite being otherwise inept in life, Giamatti's character is a savant with wine. Throughout the movie, he loses himself in the nosing and tasting of different vintages; his mind is like a catalog for wineries, grapes, and regions.

It was impressive to watch. I didn't drink wine, but it seemed to have so much more depth and character than beer. It felt like I was being challenged to up my game. Sure, it would require some education and exploration, but heck, I felt I was up to it. So I prepared to dive in.

But I had three big roadblocks in my way. First, wine does not last well for weeks in a bottle, so finishing a bottle in two days was a common occurrence for me. Sure you can buy special corks and compressed air devices, but I felt I was cheating myself out of the optimal experience by doing so. Second, that stuff is way too easy to drink. I would pour a hefty glass and then drink it like beer. And last, becoming a wine connoisseur takes passion and commitment to the product, and I had neither. It was clear that wine wouldn't be the answer, but I wasn't ready to jump back into beer either.

Then a scotch-drinking buddy suggested that we have a whiskey tasting party. I was a little surprised: this was a lifelong friend who knew about my bad experience with Tennessee whiskey. But he said, "oh, scotch is different."

Well, since I was a kid, the word 'scotch' had always had a pleasant sounding ring to it, I think mainly because I hoped it would somehow be like butterscotch. But when my father-in-law gave me a bottle of 16-year-old Chivas Regal I could only get it down my throat by diluting it in cocktails. Still, I was hunting for something new to drink—something with depth and character—so I took him up on his offer and accepted the invitation.

The rules were simple: each participant had to bring a top-, a middle-, and a bottom-shelf whiskey. They could be from any country, which allowed us to go beyond scotch. The goal was to gain exposure to a variety of new whiskeys. We would talk through each selection and compare experiences. Once the tasting was over, we could freely swap bottles if we found a mutually agreeable trading partner.

To prepare, I went straight to research. I wanted to bring a nice cross section of respectable whiskeys. As a result, I settled on a 14-year-old Glenfiddich single malt scotch whisky, a bourbon called Buffalo Trace, and a Canadian single-barrel whisky by Sazerac called Caribou Crossing. My friend had several bottles of scotch and Irish whiskey, while another friend brought only bourbon and rye whiskeys.

Happily, the whiskey didn't overload my senses. I started with the scotch, then made my way to the Irish whiskeys, and finally the bourbons and ryes. The test run was successful: by taking it slow, I made it past the first challenge of keeping the whiskey down.

But, I must admit, that from a tasting standpoint I felt like a complete rookie. There was definitely a difference between each of these spirits, but the most I could muster was "oh, that is decent" or "well, that's not quite my speed." I kept leaning on experiential terms such as smooth, harsh, or pleasant. My hope of discovering any individualized flavors or scents seemed distant. Paul Giamatti's character would not be impressed. Still, I enjoyed the experience and I knew I would be back for more.

WHY I CREATED THE KENTUCKY BOURBON EXPERIENCE PLANNING GUIDE

A few months after the tasting, I took a trip to Europe for my blog Travel Fuels Life, in which I spent two weeks hunting down James Bond movie locations. I had great fun planning that trip, which took me from Monte Carlo to Vienna—I even found the hotel from *Casino Royale* and sipped on Vesper Martinis in the bar before heading to the casino. That experience put me on the road to planning more themed trips.

When I returned to the United States, my friends suggested we have another whiskey get-together. I endeavored to take another step toward whiskey tasting mastery. But when I reached the whiskey shop, I wandered mindlessly through the aisles, getting lost in a sea of labels, and shelf tag recommendations. It was frustrating. I was lacking knowledge, and it was holding me back from making informed decisions.

I needed a crash course in bourbon. But where could I get such an education?

That's when it hit me. Kentucky is only a few hours away. Why not drive there and learn about bourbon firsthand? Immersing myself could only help with my education: I could see the process, go beyond the marketing, do the tastings, and discover my own favorites. It would also help answer those nagging questions like, does all bourbon come from Kentucky; is it the limestone water that makes it bourbon; and are older bourbons better bourbons?

Without a moment's hesitation, I started planning my trek.

The first thing I realized was that planning a whiskey distillery tour would take some special considerations. But the surprising thing was the lack of sensible planning strategies available in books or on the web. The biggest question for me was how to avoid drinking and driving. Would I need to find hotels near the distilleries? Would Uber or Lyft be available? Should I plan extra time between distilleries?

Where would I find these answers?

And choosing the distilleries I wanted to visit wasn't easy either. There are no distilleries on the map named Elijah Craig, Pappy Van Winkle, or Jefferson's. These are brand names under the umbrella of different distilleries. Sure, there were some obvious names like Maker's Mark or Buffalo Trace, but how was I to know that Eagle Rare would be found at the Buffalo Trace Distillery?

Sometimes I could find a general location for a distillery by looking at the address on the bottle, but without knowing that Henry McKenna was a Heaven Hill product its Bardstown address didn't help much; there are several distilleries in Bardstown, Kentucky.

Next I went on Google to do some searches on brand names and their parent distilleries. But this still required a large time investment. Once I found the website, I would have to type in my birth date or age and most of these forms are clunky and frustrating at best. And then, once past the gatekeeper, an Easter egg hunt would ensue. First, I had to find the brands, then compare hours, hunt down directions, and read through marketing heavy descriptions of their tours.

After going through the same process over and over on distillery site after distillery site, I would come back to a previous one, only to find the "remember me" check box that I had ticked earlier had no effect. I was back entering my birth date again.

It got so frustrating that I decided to hunt down tour companies just to ease the burden. And while their websites would tell me what groups of distilleries I could visit, I still didn't know which group was best suited for me. So I headed back to the individual distillery websites—once again entering my birth date ad nauseam.

I started checking out travel review websites. I spent most of my time reading reviews from people who had only been to one or two distilleries. You know these reviews. Most are five-star reviews with glowing remarks about how this first trip to a distillery was incredible. Honestly, who has a bad time at a distillery? (Well, there is always that rare one-star where someone has an axe to grind about the selection of whiskeys provided on a free tour.)

My biggest disappointment came from my fellow bloggers. Most had toured only a handful of distilleries, and none of them were disclosing the logistics of planning out travel between the distilleries, which left so many important questions unanswered. Did they have to get a hotel nearby? Did they Uber to the place? Did they need reservations? It was frustrating.

It soon became obvious that I would have to wing it. I started pinpointing different distilleries on Google Maps and searched things like "best Kentucky bourbon tour"—not very scientific. Then I started plotting distances, roughly sketching out a schedule, and hunting lodging nearby.

It took a few weeks of dedicated planning, but I finally ended up with a list of 19 distilleries to visit over eight days. My travels would take me mostly to Kentucky, with two stops in Tennessee on my way home. I went back to each website, gave them my birth date one more time, and completed my reservations.

This whole crazy process convinced me that Kentucky bourbon was crying out for an in-depth distillery tour planning guide.

WHY YOU WILL LOVE TOURING KENTUCKY DISTILLERIES

If I were a betting man, I would say convincing you of this will not be that difficult. Whether you like it in a cocktail, on the rocks, with a splash, or simply neat, the experience of your favorite bourbon isn't complete without getting a true sense of where it came from. Sure, you have a label to look at, but that is what a marketing department wants you to experience. After touring a distillery, I promise you, your whiskey will take on a whole new personality.

You will see the fermenters. You will remember the process. You will hear the reason they created it. You will see the barrels it came from. You might even get to draw some out with what they call a whiskey thief. There will be a comradery on the tour as you speak with fellow whiskey travelers. You will pick up scents, flavors, or sensations through a guided tasting that will change how you experience bourbon from that day forward.

The first distillery I visited raised my bourbon IQ by leaps and bounds. I learned what bourbon is and what it isn't. I could see beyond the marketing and could sense what the distillery took pride in. I heard stories of how the founders changed the course of bourbon. I tasted fermented sour mash. I took in a deep breath of the warehouse's sweet vapers—known as the angel's share—and marveled at the sheer amount of whiskey they had in storage. I learned what white dog is and had my first taste. I picked up terms like 'Kentucky hug' and 'Kentucky chew'.

And I left with a second layer of questions, like are Kentucky cows really happier because they eat the distillery's spent grains? Or was the distillery I visited really the oldest, as they claimed? It was marvelous. And it was priming me for my next trip to Kentucky.

You would think after 19 distilleries I would have grown sick of hearing about the process of making bourbon. But each distillery I visited had a different way of presenting it and there are so many layers that I was catching something new each time. It was fun to detect the subtle differences.

I don't expect you to visit as many distilleries as I did on my trip—I tend to go a little overboard when I get into research mode. But this book will definitely guide you to planning a trip of that size, if you so choose. But it will also be an invaluable guide if you only have a day in Kentucky.

My promise to you is that after reading this book you will have:

- Gained the expertise you need to plan out the logistics of a bourbon tour of Kentucky.
- A deeper knowledge of what to expect from your distillery visits, including how to approach the tastings.
- A strong foundational education on bourbon, and you will know what to listen for on your tours.
- A fun and relaxed time when you go to Kentucky, resting in the knowledge that you picked out the perfect selection of distilleries for your trip.

I hope you have such a great time that you feel compelled to reach out to me at *www.facebook.com/whiskeylore* or *www.instagram.com/whiskeylore* and that you tell me all of the best parts of your trip.

It has been a few years since I watched the movie *Sideways* but, in a roundabout way, it helped create a major shift in my appreciation for whiskey, through the example of wine. And I am glad it did.

Like wine, whiskey gives us plenty of room to explore. It helps us develop our senses of smell and taste. It connects us to the proud distillers that helped pioneer the wonderful bourbons we enjoy today. Bourbon is deeply woven into our American heritage. It gives us a wonderful conversation piece. And in a world that seems divided, it unites us as one big happy family of bourbon enthusiasts.

How To Use This Guide

When I set out to write this book, I wanted to make it an empowering resource. What I didn't want to do was create a book full of my own opinions and rankings. There are a couple of reasons for this:

First, we all have different reasons for taking this journey and every distillery I visited had its own distinct offerings and personality. Who am I to judge what may or may not appeal to you? Maybe you like history, or you want to know the science behind the spirits. Perhaps you have a passion for a brand, or you have heard a story about someone or something associated with that distillery and that alone is enough to focus your interest on that destination. Each tour is great in its own way. I want you to judge for yourself.

Second, if I tell you everything there is to know about the distillery, then I am taking away the fun of learning these things as you take the tour.

So, the first part of the book is to help give you a solid foundation of information. I'll start with a high level view of the history of bourbon, then I'll tell you how bourbon is produced, give you some of the terms you will hear while you are on your tours, and I'll help you spot marketing versus substance.

Next, I want you to have an easy time planning out your trip, so I will guide you through important considerations like whether to hire a tour guide, or conquer territories so you can get collectables, or how to plan out your own unique path through the huge variety of craft and large-scale distilleries. I'll even help you understand the regions, and the options for transportation and lodging around the various areas.

For those that are new to bourbon or who are wanting to understand how to approach the tasting portion of your tours, I have created a section that will give you tips on how to taste whiskey, the type of glass you might invest in, and the ins and outs of nosing and detecting flavor notes. I'll also define two terms you are sure to hear on your tours—Kentucky Chew and Kentucky Hug.

With this solid footing, you will be prepared to start putting together your Kentucky itinerary. This is where the last section of the book becomes an invaluable resource. You will find all the critical information you need to pick out the distilleries that are right for you. There are 32 distilleries profiled: I have based each on the distillery's standard tour.

Each profile includes maps, the focus of the tour, the brands of bourbon made there, when tours run, how to get there, special considerations, side trips, and suggestions for the next closest distilleries. I have also added a brand index to the back of the book, so you can find distilleries by the brand names you have come to know and love.

Once you determine your ultimate collection of distilleries, then you can use the links listed in the profiles to book tours yourself. Or head to ***www.whiskey-lore.com/signup***, fill in the form for a free membership, enter the promo code **bourbon1792**. That code will allow you full access to our online Kentucky distillery tour planner, including a time saving distillery wish list feature.

Have fun putting together your incredible journey but always remember...

Be Responsible.

The greatest joy in sipping bourbon is discovering its hidden depths and character. If you're looking to escape reality or crave the feeling of getting drunk this book is not for you. But, if you are curious about bourbon and want to discover the pleasures of tasting, analyzing and discovering the amazing flavors and smells "America's Native Spirit" offers, or if you love experiencing the tradition and history of distilleries, then you've come to the right place.

PART ONE
UNDERSTANDING BOURBON

"The possession of knowledge does not kill the sense of wonder and mystery. There is always more mystery."

Anaïs Nin, author

PART 1
Understanding Bourbon

You may be asking yourself, "why do I need to learn about bourbon before I go on a trip to learn about bourbon?" That is an excellent question, and I believe I have a worthy answer.

Have you ever enjoyed a movie so much that you went to see it a second time? When you watched it through again, did you suddenly notice dialog and situations that you missed the first time?

As humans, our brains are always active. We process not only the things that are happening to us, but we are also thinking ahead to what might happen next. The second time you watch a movie, your brain stops charging ahead, relaxes, and allows you to open yourself to notice additional detail.

This chapter will focus on giving you a good baseline of knowledge, so that your brain isn't constantly backing up and trying to process new concepts while the tour guide charges on to the next subject. Each distillery will have its own history and special way of producing bourbon and I want you to catch those things. I will help you understand what to listen for and what the jargon means.

And then there is the marketing. In this part of the book you'll learn that not everything you hear on a distillery tour is a proven fact. And that beyond the marketing there are the legends and myths that fill the space between the walls of those hallowed halls. You'll learn to beware of words like "best" and "oldest." These are words that have a lot of caveats or stretch the truth to its very limits. And by the time you reach your third distillery, you will start cataloging conflicting information. I'll help clarify these things ahead of time, so you can be more present during your journey.

Let's jump right into the most important question of all.

What Is Bourbon?

It was my inability to answer this simple question that made me realize that I didn't know much about bourbon. I honestly thought it was whiskey produced only in Kentucky using limestone-filtered water. The only truth in that statement is that bourbon is whiskey.

Why the misunderstanding? Well, according to the Kentucky Distillers' Association website (*www.kybourbon.com*), 95% of all bourbon produced in the United States comes from Kentucky. So that bourbon you are drinking most likely came from the Bluegrass State, but the law allows it to be made in any of the fifty states.

As for limestone water—it isn't a requirement for making bourbon, but it has advantages in the bourbon-making process. Limestone is prized for its ability to strip out the iron in water that discolors bourbon, and the calcium and magnesium it provides enhances yeast activity during fermentation. And because central Kentucky and Tennessee sit on a limestone shelf it is in plentiful supply. But many distillers, even some in Kentucky, use reverse osmosis water instead. And that doesn't break the law of what a bourbon is.

The government states that in order to use the name "bourbon" a whiskey must follow these specific rules:

- It must have a grain mixture that includes at least 51% corn.
- It cannot be distilled to over 160 proof (many distillers aim below this so they don't distill out too much flavor).
- It can only be aged in new, charred oak barrels (they do not have to be American oak).
- It cannot be any higher than 125 proof (62.5% alcohol by volume) when put into a barrel for aging.
- It must be bottled at 80 proof (40% alcohol by volume) or more.
- It must be produced in the United States of America.

You might notice that there is no age requirement in order to label a product as bourbon. It is more of a suggestion that bourbon should look and taste like bourbon to be called bourbon, regardless of age. This allows whiskey that ages quickly in smaller barrels to be labeled as bourbon.

But bourbon isn't the only word we usually see on a label. The word Kentucky often shows up in the description. As part of the definition of bourbon, a further set of standards allow each state to claim its own special moniker for their spirit. Let's look at how this works specifically for Kentucky.

KENTUCKY STRAIGHT BOURBON WHISKEY

To be labeled as Kentucky Straight Bourbon Whiskey, the following standards apply:

- The whiskey must spend its whole life in the state of Kentucky, from inception to bottling.
- If it is aged for less than four years, it must be labeled with its age.
- Any age statement requires that the youngest whiskey in the bottle is at least that age (this does not include any neutral grain spirit that is added, but the addition of this unaged spirit requires the word "blended" to be present, and the straight bourbon content must remain at 51% or greater).
- It must follow all the rules of bourbon.

BOURBON AS WHISKEY

It is said that all bourbons are whiskey, but not all whiskeys are bourbon. This is true. Whiskey is a more general term for distilled spirits. Some will argue that the difference between moonshine and whiskey is the aging process, but this is not codified in law and it leaves us some room for debate.

Another interesting element of whiskey is how it is spelled. You will see it spelled with or without an 'e' depending on which bourbon you buy. This is more a preference of the distiller, rather than a product differentiator. Most bourbon distilleries spell whiskey with an 'e' because it is an American tradition. But some founders like Bill Samuels, Sr., of Maker's Mark, wanted to pay homage to scotch whisky, which spells the word without the 'e.'

As for the grains, beyond the necessity of having 51% corn in the mash bill, the rest is up to experimentation. Rye, wheat, and malted barley are most frequently paired with corn. However, there are also bourbons using oats, quinoa, or rice.

Now that you know what bourbon is, let's check out where it came from.

A Brief History of Kentucky Bourbon

If you are a fan of history and mysteries, then bourbon is right up your alley. America's spirit is teeming with timelines, stories, heroes, disasters, and events that changed the course of American life.

It also leaves us with several questions. Who was the first to make bourbon? Where does the name come from? Which is the oldest distillery? There are questions we may never answer, and some answers that can only be made with educated guesses.

Writing a complete history of bourbon in a few pages would be a fool's errand, and it would be more information than you need to start your bourbon journey through Kentucky. There are several excellent books—as well as my Whiskey Lore podcast and website *www.whiskey-lore.com*—that cover this subject in more depth and granular detail. My focus here is to ease your curiosity, and provide a basic foundation of knowledge that will be handy during your tours.

THE ORIGINS OF WHISKEY

The history of spirit distillation goes as far back as Mesopotamia. Somewhere in the first millennium AD, grain distillation found its way to Ireland and most likely Scotland. Just like we will find with bourbon, there is no clear documentation showing when whiskey distillation began in either of these countries. This leaves us with only theories. Our ancestors prized distilled spirits for their medicinal qualities, but they also had a recreational element in those early days.

The simple reason Scotland and Ireland favored grain alcohol over brandy or other types of distillation came down to the ability to grow grains in their cold, wet climates. This distillation of available resources became a common theme, especially when distilling crossed the Atlantic Ocean to the New World.

EARLY AMERICA'S DRINK OF CHOICE

The history of whiskey in America goes all the way back to the London Company, established by King James I, who sent settlers to the colony of Virginia in 1620. These settlers were thirsty for alcohol, but shipping large quantities across the ocean was too difficult. So one of the settlers, Captain George Thorpe, began distilling whiskey for the company with the most accessible grain he could find—corn.

But the corn whiskey that eventually evolved into bourbon wasn't colonial America's first favorite. Inexpensive sugar and molasses from the Caribbean made rum the logical spirit of choice. But when England imposed the Sugar Act of 1764, the key ingredients in rum were no longer available to New Englanders. Not willing to give up on alcohol, northern farmers switched from distilling sugar cane to rye—a hearty grain that could tolerate the colder climates of the northeast. As the American Revolutionary War raged on, people began moving south and west. These areas could not sustain rye crops, but corn was readily available—this is how corn whiskey gained its roots in what would become Kentucky and Tennessee.

THE ORIGINS OF BOURBON

During the post-Revolutionary War period, Americans owed a debt of gratitude to King Louis XVI of France for providing ships and troops to defeat the British at Yorktown. To honor him, in 1785 the state government named a county in western Virginia after his royal House of Bourbon. In 1792, Bourbon County became one of the first nine counties in the newly formed state of Kentucky.

So did the name bourbon evolve from the name of the county? It is possible that the county name was being stamped on barrels before they flowed down the Mississippi River to New Orleans, but no physical evidence is available to back up this claim. And verbally, most people of the early 18th century were likely referring to the spirit simply as "corn."

The next subject for debate is the so-called "Father of Bourbon."

Around 1789, a Baptist preacher named Elijah Craig began distilling corn whiskey. There are several legends that credit him with discovering the benefits of charred oak barrels. Charring gives bourbon its distinctive color. It also imparts the vanilla and caramel components characteristic of the spirit. But just like Union General Abner Doubleday's association with the invention of baseball, the stories of a firebrand preacher creating "America's Native Spirit" are more likely fantasy and convenience, than cold, hard truth.

BOURBON GAINS ITS CHARACTER AND CONSISTENCY

Through the early 19th century, the popularity and reputation of Kentucky corn whiskey continued to grow as barrels traversed the Mississippi and Ohio Rivers. Time on the river had two important effects on bourbon: it gave it time to age, and it introduced barrel influence on the final product. A simple boat ride produced a better bourbon.

In 1823, a distiller named Oscar Pepper brought Scottish chemist Dr. James C. Crow to the banks of Glenns Creek in Kentucky. His hope was to greatly increase the quality of his whiskey. In those early days of American whiskey production, the quality of the spirit often varied from batch to batch. Dr. Crow realized that by adding mash from a previous fermentation to a newer batch, he would achieve much needed consistency. This technique is known as the sour mash process.

THE FIRST BOURBON BOOM

Despite a growing market for corn whiskey, it wasn't until the arrival of an invention by Irishman Aeneas Coffey, that American distillers were able to increase production to meet demand. Before 1830, distillers had to create spirits batch by batch using the same pot stills as their forefathers, a laborious process with a lot of stopping and starting. The arrival of the Coffey column still allowed distillation to continue uninterrupted. This was a key factor in bringing on the era of mass production of spirits on both sides of the Atlantic.

By the mid 1850s, bourbon was making a name for itself. Things looked bright for the assortment of distillers popping up across Kentucky, but the Civil War stunted their growth. Grain was needed for food in the Confederacy, so several Southern states banned alcohol sales and production. Then a Union blockade of the Mississippi cut off the flow of bourbon to New Orleans. Another dagger came from President Lincoln, who raised taxes on whiskey to help fund the war effort.

But as America recovered from the devastation of war, expanding railways and industrial production helped refuel bourbon's rise. It is from this era that many of today's most notable Kentucky distillers trace their roots.

KENTUCKY PROTECTS BOURBON

The bourbon boom brought on both success and greed. One of the most notorious players in the industry started out as a small distillation company from Peoria, Illinois. They were soon merging with and buying up distilleries all across the country—sometimes using physical intimidation or the point of a gun to get the job done. Known as the Whiskey Trust, in time they came to produce almost 75% of the whiskey sold in the United States. And much of it was of questionable quality.

As early as 1870, Kentucky producers took action to protect their product's reputation. George Garvin Brown began bottling and sealing his Old Forester bourbon to prevent tampering. Colonel Edmund H. Taylor went a step further by lobbying the United States

Congress to enact tougher standards for whiskey. This culminated in the Bottled-in-Bond Act of 1897, America's first consumer protection law.

A decade later, another consumer protection law unsettled and confused the whiskey industry. The intent of the Pure Food and Drug Act of 1906 was to define words like "pure" and "straight," but instead it created a marketing frenzy because those terms were so poorly defined in the law. In 1909, it took the president of the United States William Howard Taft to solidify the terminology for whiskey going forward. Known today as the Taft Decision, it provided the industry with definitions for "straight whiskey," "blended whiskey" (straight whiskey mixed with a neutral grain spirit), and "imitation whiskey."

TEMPERANCE AND PROHIBITION

Perhaps unsurprisingly, the rise in whiskey's popularity also caused a rise in drunkenness. Families were feeling the pain as fathers would throw away their paychecks at the saloon, or bring their drunken rages into the home. This brought about the Temperance Movement. Teetotallers and organizations like The American Temperance Society banded together to find a solution. Their initial focus was just on the reduction of alcohol use, but soon they graduated to pushing for all-out abstinence.

By shifting their focus to political channels, the movement moved from suggestion to law. In 1851, Maine became the first state to prohibit the manufacturing or sale of alcoholic beverages, with several states following suit. In 1881, Kansas became the first state to ban consumption of alcohol, adding it to the state's constitution. The Anti-Saloon League began lobbying nationwide in the early 20th century, and soon voters were choosing between "wet" or "dry" political candidates.

It was around this time that a hatchet-wielding reformer from Kentucky named Carrie Nation began taking her rage out on saloons across the Midwest. Her memorable campaign terrorized saloon owners across the country.

When the United States entered World War I, there was little opposition to mandated wartime prohibition. By this point, 33 states (including Kentucky) had already enacted their own form of prohibition. The 18th Amendment sailed through with ease. Only Rhode Island and Connecticut abstained from ratification, and the Volstead Act was set to clamp down on everything from whiskey to beer to wine.

So what happened to the bourbon industry during Prohibition? Luckily, the government saw the need for medicinal whiskey, leaving a crack in the door for six companies. Four of those licensed distilleries were in Kentucky. These included Frankfort (now Four Roses), A. Ph. Stitzel (Old Fitzgerald), Brown-Forman (Old Forester, Early Times), and the Glenmore Distillery (now owned by Sazerac). These companies could sell and store whiskey, but they weren't allowed to produce new whiskey.

As for other distillers, they did what they could to stay afloat. Jim Beam, for example, bought a citrus farm in Florida and a rock quarry in Clermont, Kentucky that would later become the new home of his family's whiskey after Prohibition. But most pre-Prohibition distillers shuttered their doors permanently.

As for everyday Americans, Prohibition turned them into common criminals, looking for any way possible to circumvent the alcohol laws. Moonshiners were taking to the hills and midnight distilling. The rise of bootleggers led to mob activity. A shortage of whiskey led to deaths and paralysis from adulterated whiskey, while another unintended consequence of Prohibition was the introduction of women to drinking culture. Ultimately, the "noble experiment" ended up glorifying alcohol rather than stopping it's consumption.

After its thirteen-year run, Prohibition ended with an unceremonious thud. The only positive? A country buried deep in the Depression could legally have a drink.

POST PROHIBITION TO THE 21ST CENTURY

The bourbon-loving public was hungry for whiskey, but the distillers that survived Prohibition had little to sell. Ramping up production required family-owned distilleries to seek outside investment. And stores of medicinal whiskey had been exhausted, so distillers had to become creative with what they produced while they waited for their bourbon to age.

The Depression and Prohibition also put hardships on bourbon industry suppliers. For example, the reduced demand for barrels from the timber industry and coopers put a strain on their revenues. It has been suggested that a mighty cooper's union was behind a 1938 ruling by the Alcohol and Tobacco Tax and Trade Bureau that producers must age bourbon only in new, charred oak barrels—a little self preservation. Interestingly enough, this theory is touted more on scotch whisky tours than it is on bourbon tours.

Unlike World War I, distilleries found plenty of work during World War II. The government needed industrial alcohol for antifreeze, lacquer, pesticides, and other uses, making distilleries shift to wartime production. But by the close of the war, there was a shortage of sipping whiskey, so distillers ramped up production. This created a bourbon boom that lasted through the 1950s, but overproduction flooded the market with whiskey. Distillers were forced to cut their prices and by the mid-1960s bourbon had fallen out of favor with a younger generation that saw the spirit as their father's drink. It wouldn't be until the second decade of the 21st century before the mass appeal of bourbon returned.

Today, bourbon fills social media with people doing tastings, comparisons, swapping bottles, and featuring bourbon in Tinder poses on the beach or in front of the Eiffel Tower. Distillers feed the thirst for bourbon by producing barrel proof, small batch, single barrel, limited editions, and Bottled-in-Bond versions. Stalwart distilleries like Buffalo Trace, Jim Beam, and Four Roses are ramping up their capacities and building new warehouses. Craft distilleries are sourcing spirits from other distilleries so they can speed product to market. Old brands like Kentucky Owl, James E. Pepper, and Yellowstone are being revived, while creative new distilleries like Rabbit Hole, Neeley Family Distilling, or Kentucky Artisan Distilling are pushing the boundaries of what bourbon can be.

After many booms and busts through the years, it looks like bourbon is finally standing on solid ground.

HISTORY EXTRA: WHO'S THE OLDEST?

When you start your travels it will amaze you how many distilleries claim to be the first or the oldest.

Woodford Reserve claims they are the oldest distillery site. Hmmm, so does Buffalo Trace. There is even a third distillery that makes this same claim. Who is really the oldest? It all depends on how you split hairs. Let's investigate.

When you visit Woodford Reserve, they will point out the buildings that started as the Old Oscar Pepper Distillery in 1838. Remember, this is where Dr. James C. Crow came to institute the sour mash process. Oscar Pepper's father Elijah Pepper had a legacy of distilling dating back to 1780, but that was back in central Virginia. It wasn't until 1790 that he settled in what would become Kentucky. And it wasn't until 1812 that Elijah would begin distilling on the site of the modern Woodford Reserve Distillery. Does that live up to its claim of being the oldest site?

Buffalo Trace would take issue with that. They claim that Hancock and Willis Lee were distilling on their site in 1775. However, as America was not yet a country at this point, this cannot be verified by tax records. It wasn't until 1812 that Harrison Blanton built the first distillery on the site. If that year sounds familiar, it should. It is the same year Elijah Pepper started his distillery.

So, let's inspect the words Buffalo Trace uses. Their website suggests they are the "oldest continuously operating distillery." They base this off the claim that "during Prohibition the distillery was ... permitted to remain operational, to make whiskey for 'medicinal purposes.'" But think back to our history lesson—by law, no distillery could make new whiskey during Prohibition. It's a subtle fact that is easily missed. The reality is, it took a distiller's holiday in 1928 to open the door to distillation of new medicinal whiskey, but only A. Ph. Stitzel still had enough equipment available to do so at that time. But Stitzel-Weller couldn't be the oldest continuously running distillery because their current site no longer actively produces bourbon. Confused yet?

So which is the oldest distillery in Kentucky? How about Maker's Mark? They went so far as to get the stamp of approval from the *Guinness Book of World Records*.

The company has two potential claims.

First, it is said some manner of distilling started in 1773 on the site where Maker's Mark now stands. But what was being distilled? There was no record or firm date. We will leave that one to legend until they uncover further evidence.

The second claim dates back to 1805: this is when the first public record shows Charles Burks building a grist mill on the site. But what year did distilling start? They convinced Guinness, but I remain a skeptic.

I'm sorry I can't give you a definitive answer. But the reason I took you through this exercise is to show how these claims are very hard to prove. Just like the origins of the name bourbon, or the person who first distilled something similar to what we call bourbon today, some things will remain a mystery.

Just for fun, let's look at some other "oldest" and "first" claims. Old Forester is referred to as the oldest continuous running bourbon brand, dating back to 1870. This goes back to Prohibition when only about ten brands were being distributed for medicinal use. This claim is probably the most accurate of any listed so far, although let me split some more hairs—the brand was originally spelled Old Forrester (note the extra "r"), so it isn't exactly the same brand. Two can play at this game!

When you hear the name Evan Williams, you will hear the claim he is "Kentucky's 1st distiller." In a countryside filled with Scotch-Irish immigrants this seems a little hard to prove. But a historical marker clarifies saying he was the first "commercial" distiller, starting operations in Louisville in 1783. But this was nine years before Kentucky was a state. And a short lived Kentucky County, Virginia had disappeared by 1780. So he was actually distilling in what was then Jefferson County, Virginia, not Kentucky.

I could go on for hours. And actually, I do. If you love hearing these mysteries dissected and uncovered, check out the Whiskey Lore podcast on Apple Podcasts, Google Podcasts, Spotify, or your favorite podcast app. Or just go to *www.whiskey-lore.com* click on the episodes link and listen online. From determining the "Father of Bourbon" to understanding where Bottled-in-Bond came from, it will give you plenty of food for thought.

Bourbon Production in a Nutshell

The one question I always hear when I tell people how many distilleries I've been to is "aren't you sick of hearing about the distillation process?" In a word, no.

The process is part of the reason each distillery visit is so unique. Hidden between the fermenters and cookers are the little nuggets that separate one distillery or bourbon from another. Yes, the basic process is similar from one distillery to the next, but the equipment isn't the same; the fermentation times aren't the same; the mash bills aren't the same; the warehouses aren't the same; the philosophies aren't the same, and so on.

This is where the book you are reading now is going to give you a leg up on the rest of your tour party. While they are trying to grasp the basics of bourbon production and distillation, you will be absorbing all of the subtle nuances. And all that I talk about here will come alive before your eyes.

Don't worry, this isn't a chemistry lesson. I will keep to the basics and will give you just enough information to enhance your experience. I'll also give you some suggestions of things to specifically listen for during your tour.

MILLING AND MASH BILLS

Bourbon production starts with a choice of grains, one of which has to be corn. As you will recall, bourbon requires at least 51% corn in its grain recipe—this is called a mash bill. Every distillery will have its own unique mash bill or set of mash bills. Some distilleries like to keep their mash bills a secret, like the formula for Coca-Cola. But most are very open about it. When the tour guide starts talking about percentages of corn, malted barley, and other grains, that is their mash bill.

Some distilleries, including Four Roses and Bulleit, have several mash bills. Along with corn and malted barley, most bourbons contain rye or wheat as a third grain. Rye is the most popular and tends to give bourbon a robust, spicy characteristic. Wheated bourbons tend to be softer and more earthy. Some distilleries are stretching beyond these standard grains by using rice, oats, and quinoa. And others are experimenting with four-grain and five-grain bourbons.

When your guide talks about mash bills, you may hear these terms:

High Rye Mash Bill
Don't let the emphasis on the word rye throw you off. This is still a bourbon, meaning it still contains 51% corn. The majority of bourbons are made using rye in their mash bills. However, in a high rye bourbon the total amount of rye in the recipe reaches over 15%. Basil Hayden and Bookers are examples of high rye bourbons. Both bourbons contain 27% rye in their mash bills.

Rye Whiskey
A rye whiskey is not a bourbon. Rye whiskey has a mash bill featuring at least 51% rye. Sazerac Rye, Knob Creek Rye, and Rittenhouse Rye are examples of rye whiskey.

Wheated Mash Bill
Like high rye, this term refers to a bourbon variation. In this recipe wheat is elevated to over 15% of the total mash bill, while still containing at least 51% corn. Maker's Mark and Rebel Yell are wheated bourbon as they include 18% and 20% wheat respectively in their mash bills.

Wheat Whiskey

A wheat whiskey is not a bourbon. Wheat whiskey has a mash bill featuring at least 51% wheat. Bernheim Original is an example of a wheat whiskey, with 51% wheat in its mash bill.

Once the mash bill is determined, a few distilleries mill the grains together; most have them milled separately because corn cooks at higher temperatures than barley, wheat, and rye. Milling is not always done on-site—if it is, listen for the type of mill they use. The two most popular are hammer mills and roller mills.

Side note: *Some distilleries will limit or prevent the use of cameras or cellphones in their facilities because of insurance limitations and the risk of explosions. But the greatest danger of sparks might not be where you think. Warehouses filled with angel's share and still rooms cooking alcohol at high temperatures aren't as potentially dangerous as the mill room, which has highly combustible flour dust floating in the air. Just a small spark could set off a mighty explosion.*

MASHING

The next step is to add water to the milled grains. Corn is usually the first ingredient added to the cooker, followed by barley and the additional grain(s). Next, the mixture goes into the fermentation tanks. At this stage, the mixture cools to under 90°F to prepare for the addition of yeast. Any warmer and the yeast would die.

Next, most distilleries start the sour mash process. Here they add leftover mash from the previous batch, referred to as setback or backset, and add it to the cooked grains. This creates batch consistency. Just like with sourdough bread, it works like a starter, and its higher PH level helps the yeast fight off bacteria that can ruin the batch.

Pay attention because a few distilleries use the sweet mash process, which they say helps add more flavor and character to the bourbon. However, the lower PH levels make sweet mash much more difficult to make, because of the added risk of bacteria and contamination. When reviewing distillery profiles for your own trip, you will notice there are three in the state that use the sweet mash process. Is it really a better process for a better tasting bourbon? When you're doing your tasting, you can judge for yourself.

Once the cooked grains and setback are married together, yeast is blended into the mixture. Yeast comes in both liquid and dry form. Some distilleries simply purchase distillers yeast. But there are several distilleries that pride themselves on having their own proprietary yeast strain. Some yeast strains go back generations.

How much influence the yeast has on the flavor notes of bourbon is up for debate. And it's a great question for your tour guide.

FERMENTATION

If you are at a distillery that has open-top fermenters, this will be your first chance to actually see and maybe even taste the product. However, some distilleries use closed-top stainless steel fermenters. They suggest this helps keep contamination issues to a minimum, while others say that open-tops are useful for attracting wild yeast strains present in the atmosphere.

Distillers use either wooden or stainless steel fermenters. Again, it is fun to ask the tour guide's opinion, is wood better than stainless steel? You will be surprised at the varied responses. That is why tours at Neeley Family Distillery in Kentucky or Laphroaig in Scotland are so interesting. They both use a combination of wood and stainless steel in the same facility, for different reasons. So if anyone would know which is better, they would.

Another variable between distilleries is how much time they allow their mash to ferment. Distilleries have different theories on how the length of fermentation time affects the bourbon. The average fermentation time is around 72 hours, but some distilleries will stretch fermentation to pull out additional flavors.

If open-top fermenters are being used, notice how the mash looks different in each. One fermenter may be at one day, the next at two, and so on. If you can, put your hand above the mash and feel the heat. This is a natural heat being generated as the yeast feeds on the sugar and creates alcohol and carbon dioxide. But don't stick your head too far into the fermenter; the carbon dioxide is potent and can literally take your breath away. Depending on the distillery, they may allow you to dip your finger in and sample the mash. Notice how just a couple of days of fermentation turns it from sweet to sour.

When the fermentation stage is complete, they drain off the liquid and send it to the still for distillation. A portion of the leftover spent grain or slop becomes setback for the next batch. The remaining slop usually goes to local farmers, who use it as a protein-rich supplement for their livestock. This is where the most overused joke on distillery tours will occur. They imply that Kentucky's cows are happier than anywhere else because they are eating the distillery's spent grains. It is not because it contains alcohol: there is only a negligible amount in the leftover mash. If they are happier, it is because of the added protein in their diet.

If you want to hear more about why giving cows too much spent grain is a bad thing, check out the Whiskey Lore Season One episode The Origins of Bottled-in-Bond.

DISTILLATION

Thanks to the yeast, we now have a fermented liquid that sits at five to ten percent alcohol by volume. To raise that alcohol level, the distiller uses a combination of stills. There are two primary types of stills used for the first distillation.

Continuously running column stills are popular in Kentucky because of their mass production capabilities. You can identify most column stills by their height—the majority are two to three stories tall. Shaped like a tall musical flute, they contain little portholes that show the liquid working its way down and the steam rising inside the still. The fermented liquid heats to a temperature between the boiling point of alcohol (173°F), and water (212°F). The alcohol vapor climbs and escapes from the top of the still while the liquid drops through hole-filled shelves to the bottom.

Pot stills are more traditional and produce spirits in batches. Some look like copper Hershey's Kisses or genie bottles, but they can also look very industrial. Pot stills are popular in Scotland and Ireland, and used frequently by smaller craft distilleries. They are hollow vessels that use a heating source at their base to raise the temperature of the liquid. The alcohol escapes out of the top through a stem. With endless varieties of shapes and sizes, pot stills impart more influence on the flavor and body of a spirit than their more standardized cousins, the column still.

Whether using a pot still or column still, the result is a spirit between 50 and 60% alcohol by volume. We call the resulting spirit low wine.

To increase the alcohol even further, the low wine is distilled a second time using a doubler or thumper.

A doubler is a pot still that requires the first run of distillate to run through a condenser to turn it back into a liquid before being redistilled.

A thumper, on the other hand, accepts vapor and does not require condensing between distillations, thus speeding the process. The name thumper comes from the noise the still makes as it accepts the hot vapors.

The second distillation removes impurities and increases the amount of alcohol to around 63 to 70%. We call the resulting spirit a new make or white dog.

> **Side note:** *White dog is not vodka, but it is close. Vodka is a pure spirit that should be flavorless, so it requires the spirit to go through more distillations than white dog. Gin is similar to vodka, with the additional step of infusing botanicals. Many new bourbon distilleries produce moonshine, gin, and vodka because of the similarity in production and equipment to making bourbon. This gives them something to sell while their bourbon ages.*

Other important pieces of equipment that you may see during the distillation process are tanks labeled heads and tails.

Heads are the spirits that come from the beginning of the distillation (or run). This alcohol is mostly methanol and if consumed can lead to blindness and even death. During Prohibition, some rookie distillers left this byproduct in their spirit, making it poisonous— thus the stories of people going blind from drinking whiskey.

We call the middle of the run the hearts; this is the choice spirit that goes into the barrels to age.

The tails are the leftovers after the hearts have run. Tails are low in alcohol and don't always taste pleasant. Distillers will discard them or use them as cleaning agents. I've even heard of one distiller that uses the tails to proof down their spirits, instead of using water.

In Scotland, heads and tails are usually mixed together and redistilled with new spirits. But unlike the sour mash process with bourbon, this is more about reducing waste rather than creating consistency. Some bourbon distillers have adopted this technique as well.

AGING

Before the new make spirit is put into a barrel, by law, it must be reduced to 125 proof (62.5% alcohol by volume). This is normally done with reverse-osmosis water.

The spirits are then injected into new charred oak barrels through a hose. In many cases, this mimics taking a gasoline nozzle and sticking it into a gas tank. Most bourbon distilleries use American oak, but other forms of oak are acceptable.

Old Forester in Louisville is the only distillery tour in Kentucky where an on-site cooper assembles and fires new oak barrels right before your eyes, though a few distilleries have on-site coopers for repairing damaged or leaking barrels. But if you want to see the entire process of barrel production, I urge you to tour Kentucky Cooperage (Independent Stave Company) in Lebanon, KY.

Something to listen for at the distillery is the level of char used on the barrels. Level 1 is the equivalent of toasting, with the barrel being fired for only 15 seconds. Level 4 can see the barrel being fired for as long as 55 seconds, creating an alligatoring effect and bringing more of the wood characteristics to the bourbon. Most distilleries use between a level 3 and level 4 char.

Hopefully you will be lucky enough to see a cask being filled. So far, New Riff is the only distillery where I had this honor and it was mostly due to timing and the location of their tasting room.

Next, it's time for my favorite part of the tour: the warehouse. Here you will experience the most pleasant smell of the entire tour, called the angel's share. And while it has a wonderful sounding name and scent, in reality, it is the smell of bourbon being lost through evaporation. Some barrels lose upwards of five percent of their contents to the angels, every year.

But more happens in the aging process than just evaporation. Because Kentucky has frequent shifts between hot and cold weather, the wood of the barrels expands and contracts, soaking in and pushing out whiskey from the oak. This speeds up the aging process. Scotland, on the other hand, has more subtle changes in weather so wood interaction is less aggressive and aging happens over a longer period of time. This is why bourbon is considered mature at younger ages than scotch.

The sweet spot for many bourbons is between five to nine years in a barrel. But much depends on the way the whiskey is stored. Bourbon stored on the top floor of a seven-story warehouse (also known as a rickhouse) will age much faster than bourbon near the floor. And some distilleries use shorter warehouses to produce a more even result from top to bottom.

Every distillery will have their own unique methods and it's fun to discover how they store a high-quality bourbon versus bottom-shelf brands. But be aware that not all distilleries age their bourbons on-site so not all tours will take you into a warehouse.

Check out the profiles in this book or at *www.whiskey-lore.com/distilleries* and log in to see if a visit to the warehouse is included on the distillery's standard tour.

BOTTLING

When a bourbon has reached its desired age, the cork (referred to as a bung cork) is removed and they dump the contents of the barrel into a trough where unwanted char remnants are left behind. Only a few distilleries show the area where this is done. Sometimes tours like Jim Beam American Stillhouse will allow someone on the tour to catch some bourbon as it leaves the barrel. This isn't always the case, so be prepared to volunteer if the opportunity presents itself.

Something you probably won't see is when they send the bourbon through a chill filtering process. In this step, the whiskey is chilled to around -15 to -25°F and poured through particle filters. The process removes any unwanted protein molecules and debris from the bourbon; it also prevents cloudy or hazy bourbon. Unfortunately, chill filtering also removes flavorful oils. There is a movement where distillers are skipping the filtering process to enhance the flavor of their bourbons. If you want to experiment with some of these, look for bottles labeled "non-chill filtered."

The final step before bottling is the combining of barrel contents and proofing down. However, some bourbons go into the bottle at cask strength or are bottled directly from a single barrel.

Here are some terms you may encounter in your local whiskey shop:

Small Batch
There is no legal definition for how many barrels constitutes a small batch. So marketing departments use this term on anything from a two barrel marriage up to thousands of barrels.

Single Barrel
This means the contents of the bottle came from a single barrel of bourbon. This can create some inconsistencies from bottle to bottle, but many people enjoy drinking one bourbon from a single source. Usually these bourbons will have markings telling you the specific barrel it came from. It could also have a code telling you where it came from in the warehouse.

Cask Strength or Barrel Proof
This means no proofing took place during the bottling process. You are drinking exactly what came out of the barrel(s). Because the proof changes as a bourbon ages, many of these bourbons will have the proof handwritten on the label.

Bottled-in-Bond
This is a legal definition that was created by the government in 1897. It requires a spirit to be stored in a government-bonded warehouse for four years; it must be bottled at 100 proof, and there are other legal standards as well. This is not just a marketing term, it was a classification developed to give government assurance of a spirit's quality.

Many large distilleries bottle off-site and out of view. Craft distilleries sometimes have the bottling done in the same room as the distillation process. Buffalo Trace uses machines to bottle many of their bourbons, but on the tour you get to see Blanton's bourbon hand bottled. At Maker's Mark, you see them hand dipping bottles in red wax; and you can even dip your own, for an extra fee.

So have I got you excited to start planning your Kentucky bourbon experience? Believe me, I have just given you a taste. If I sucked you in with the brief history of bourbon, then the profiles will help you find the distilleries that have a heavy focus on history. If you are fascinated by the process, then the profiles will point out distilleries that put an emphasis on the detail and science of distilling.

But before you jump too far ahead, it's time for me to give you the tools that will help you nail down the perfect plan for your getaway. Are you ready?

PART TWO
PLANNING YOUR ADVENTURE

~~~~~~~~~~~~~~~~~~~~~~~~~~

"Once the travel bug bites there is no known antidote, and I know that I shall be happily infected until the end of my life."

Michael Palin, actor and author

PART 2
Planning Your Adventure

So many distilleries, so little time! Which one will you visit first? How many should you plan to tour? What is the best way to get around? Can you really plan this all out yourself, or should you hire a tour guide?

Personally, I love planning out adventures. When it comes to travel, my initials should be DIY. If you are the same, then this section will give you all the tools you need to plan your Kentucky bourbon experience. But maybe you would rather hire a tour guide to take the pressure off, or maybe you are on the fence about what to do. Whichever way you are leaning, this section should help you make educated decisions, so you get the most out of your travel time.

By the end of this chapter you will:

- Understand the logistics involved in a do-it-yourself plan.
- Know the different strategies for conquering trails and regions.
- Know how to choose between craft and larger distilleries.
- Have strategies for paring down your list to the perfect "must-see" distilleries.
- Know how many distilleries you can visit in a day.
- Know how to get around Kentucky (and safely!) to the distilleries.
- Know how to plan accommodations.
- Be ready to use the profiles in the back of the book to plan your adventure.

As you reach the end of this chapter, I will have you armed with all the information you need to nail down your own personalized Kentucky bourbon experience, using the distillery profiles at the end of the book as your guide.

Travel Choices

When I was planning my first solo adventure to Kentucky, avoiding drinking and driving was my number one concern. I wasn't sure how much alcohol I would consume at each distillery, and I wasn't sure if Uber or Lyft would be options in the more rural areas of the state. I almost hired a tour company just so I could get the experience without worrying about getting around. But I decided to roll on and keep my schedule conservative. You will have the advantage of my experience, so you can hire a tour guide because you want to, rather than doing it through fear.

GOING BY TOUR GUIDE

There are many advantages to hiring a tour guide. Tours can be a great way to meet other whiskey enthusiasts and enjoy the day without having to put your hands on the wheel. Tour guides sometimes provide extra perks and experiences, because they have established a special relationship with a distillery. They are experts that can provide additional commentary and history as you travel between destinations. And most tours provide a packaged lunch or special dining experience along the way.

Drawbacks to tours include less flexibility, a slower pace, and higher costs. From a planning standpoint, if they have multiple tour paths you still need to know how to choose between the groups of distilleries in each package. So, if you plan to hire a tour guide, keep this book and its profiles handy to help you make informed decisions.

> *Side note:* If you go with a guided tour, make sure to confirm whether the cost of the guide also includes the entry fee to the distilleries. This is not always the case.

There are several tour companies that provide bourbon tour experiences. I have not used these companies myself, but they get good social media reviews. Make sure to do your own research. If you are interested, ask about potentially customizing your tour.

Blue Grass Tours
www.bluegrasstours.com

Bourbon City Cruisers (Louisville)
www.bourboncitycruisers.com

Bourbon Boat
www.kyrivertours.com

Central Kentucky Tours
www.centralkentuckytours.com

Ken Tucky Tours
www.kentuckytoursktt.com

Mint Julep Experiences: Louisville
www.mintjuleptours.com

Pegasus Distillery Experiences
www.takepegasusdistilled.com

DO-IT-YOURSELF

If you want flexibility, there is no better way to plan a Kentucky bourbon experience than to do-it-yourself. Planning your own trip allows you to choose the specific distilleries you want to visit, collect stamps or coins if you want to, fit in side trips, and experience Kentucky in your own sweet time. But perhaps the best part of DIY planning is getting to cherry pick the distilleries that fit your personality.

I have also had some nice surprises by planning out trips myself.

Because I like to travel in the morning and in the off-season, I have had many instances where I was the only one on the tour and, as a result, received the VIP treatment. Or where the tour guide, on finding out that I already knew about the process of making bourbon, focused the tour on additional behind-the-scenes information, going completely off script. I have also had opportunities to fill up a water bottle with bourbon, talk directly to a distiller, and taste the product straight from the barrel.

The drawbacks to DIY include finding the time to plan, potential planning inexperience, transportation worries, and listening to the same old music in the car instead of a tour agent who will provide you with whiskey stories and anecdotes.

That said, keep reading because we will solve the first three issues in the next few pages. And I can't recommend highly enough (though I might be extremely biased) that you replace the dusty old tunes with downloaded episodes of the Whiskey Lore podcast to supplement your bourbon knowledge.

Okay, enough with the personal plugs. Before I help you pick out your dream list of distilleries, let's see some options you may want to consider, which can net you some serious swag along the way.

The Kentucky Bourbon Trail®

If you are like me, two or three distilleries just won't tame your appetite for Kentucky bourbon. The Kentucky Distillers' Association knows there are many people just like us, so they created The Kentucky Bourbon Trail®. Visit *www.kybourbontrail.com* to find the list of participating distilleries, and get your official free souvenir passport—you'll then collect stamps along the way as you visit distilleries, and can claim your gift once you've completed the trail.

The Kentucky Distillers' Association suggests that you can do all 18 distilleries in four days.

But don't lock yourself into just visiting the big distilleries. There is also an official **Kentucky Bourbon Trail Craft Tour®** with 19 additional distilleries to conquer. Now, if that sounds like a daunting task, don't worry. You can take on the trail in bite-sizes by conquering smaller regions one by one. First, buy the $3 passport book at any of the official member distilleries and then collect the stamps as you conquer each. When you finish a region, you get a souvenir coin. Finish all four regions and you get a decorative barrel stave to place your coins on, as well as a branded tasting glass. If you are bold and want to conquer this tour in one trip, make sure to plan at least a week and a half.

Keep in mind that the trails focus on specific member distilleries—there are, of course, more than just these 37 distilleries in the state. Know that the trail lists may shift or grow over time. And understand that these are suggested paths rather than tours—the Kentucky Distillers' Association does not provide guides or transportation. Ultimately, this is just another fun way to do-it-yourself.

Stateline Distillery Tour (Western Kentucky)

Because Kentucky is a long state, planning a trip out to western Kentucky can be a challenge. But three distilleries in Kentucky and Tennessee have banded together to make it worth your time. Visit Old Glory Distillery (in Clarksville, TN), MB Roland Distillery, and the Casey Jones Distillery and each will reward you with a nice branded shot glass. Get a stamp at each location and when you reach the third distillery you will receive a nice wooden stave to display your shot glasses. These distilleries are within miles of each other, so it is possible to complete this tour in one day.
Visit *www.statelinewhiskeytour.com* for more information.

The B-Line (Northern Kentucky)

We bourbon enthusiasts don't live by bourbon tours alone. If you are planning to be in northern Kentucky near Cincinnati, check out the B-Line. This combination of distilleries, bars, and restaurants will offer you swag for conquering a portion of the B-Line.
Visit *www.findyoursippingpoint.com/do-the-line* for more information.

Louisville Urban Bourbon Trail (Louisville Area)

Visiting Louisville? All you'll need is six stamps from the area's 40+ participating restaurants, bars, and distilleries to get a t-shirt.
Visit *www.bourboncountry.com/things-to-do/urban-bourbon-trail* for more information.

Creative Ways to Choose Distillery Tours

One thing that was apparent when I toured distilleries across Kentucky—there is a distillery for everyone. The challenge is finding the one that speaks to you.

The easiest way is to find the name of a distillery or brand you are familiar with and just go there. But what is the fun of trying something you already know? It is time to stretch yourself and use this opportunity to discover some new favorites and enjoy some new experiences. Whether you're into historic distilleries, chocolate pairing, sensory experiences, women's history, ghost stories, crafted cocktails, or smelling the angel's share, you will find a distillery suited to what you love.

SIZE CONSIDERATIONS

There is a major temptation to just go with the well-established names you know. There is nothing wrong with that. But if you are planning on visiting two or more distilleries, a mix of large and craft distilleries will give you an appreciation for all that Kentucky has to offer.

Large Distilleries

If you want to see what a large production facility looks like, head to Wild Turkey or the new Bulleit facility in Shelbyville. These distilleries are so large that you need a bus to get between buildings. Large distilleries will help you understand how some facilities produce huge volumes of whiskey. The amount of whiskey these operations produce in a day is staggering. However, due to their sheer size, these large distilleries sometimes only show you a portion of the process.

That said, not all large distillery tours are the same. It surprised me to find that the Jim Beam American Stillhouse Tour shows you elements of the larger distillery and also a smaller craft size distillery within the same tour. Meanwhile, Old Forester is another large producer but their downtown Louisville facility has a very small footprint, while still showing almost the entire bourbon making process.

The one thing that is most consistent between larger distilleries is how polished the tours are. But don't think, just because they are corporate, they are devoid of personality. Companies like Beam Suntory, Brown-Forman, Diageo, and Sazerac do a wonderful job of letting their historic distilleries keep their personalities.

Craft Distilleries

Just like large distilleries, craft distilleries are not all the same. If you think craft distillery means small, simple, and limited, think again. While smaller distilleries may not produce the volumes the larger distilleries do, there are some very successful craft distilleries that pride themselves on their polished operations.

Many craft distilleries have aspirations of becoming large distilleries, while some may hope to be acquired by a larger distillery. And others love being small craft distilleries and embrace the creativity and freedom to work in a smaller, less structured environment.

Craft distillery tours can range from polished to ad hoc. A craft tour is a great opportunity to walk the floor of the distillery, or maybe meet the master distiller, taste the sour mash, or draw whiskey straight from the barrel.

As you create your perfect wish list of distilleries, don't focus too much on size. As you will find, there are many other considerations ahead that will take precedent. But once you have a list nailed down, make sure you have at least one craft and one large distillery in your final plans. This will keep you from getting a one dimensional view of Kentucky bourbon.

Side note: So what constitutes a craft distillery? According to the American Craft Spirits Association, a craft distillery is independently owned and operated, and the distiller must have at least 75% equity stake in their company. In addition, the distillery must produce under 750,000 gallons of spirits a year.

CONQUERING A REGION

Kentucky is a deceptively long state, so when trip planning you'll need to think about how far—and for how long—you're willing to travel. Traveling from one end of the state to the other might force you to be in the car more than you want to be.

I'd recommend instead picking a region and spending a day or two enjoying the best that area has to offer. In this guide, I have created a series of six logical regions that are manageable enough that you should be able to schedule at least three tours per day.

Here are the regions I cover in the distillery profiles:

Bardstown
Known as the Bourbon Capital of the World, you will find a large selection of distilleries within a short drive of this quaint little town. If you are planning multiple days in the state, Bardstown should be at the top of your list.

Central
The area between Lexington and Louisville contains some of the most iconic distilleries in the state, and is also exploding with a large variety of craft distilleries. Note that this region includes Lawrenceburg and Frankfort.

Lexington

Known as a destination for horse farms and fans of Kentucky Wildcat basketball, this town features plenty of distillery options—including the Lexington Distillery District. Located near two main Interstate Highways, the area gives you a convenient way to experience your first distillery tour.

Louisville

Recently, the downtown thoroughfare known as Whiskey Row has seen a major revival and there are several distilleries on this main drag to choose from. This is a great place to spend one, two, or even three days, either on foot or by taking advantage of Uber and Lyft.

North

This part of the state may not be too familiar to bourbon fans, but from Covington and Cincinnati you can head east or south and find a growing group of craft distilleries.

West

The most spread out region in Kentucky, it is easy to neglect these distilleries. But if you want some great history, tastes, lower-priced tours, and smaller crowds then this is the land of hidden gems.

CREATING YOUR SHORT LIST OF DISTILLERIES

With the considerations of region and distillery sizes in the back of your mind, it is time to take on the entire state of Kentucky and start sketching out a list of distilleries that you want to visit.

Normally, this would be a daunting task and most people would default to looking up distillery names that are familiar. But I am about to empower you with a more personalized and logical way of picking your final list.

Let me start by saying that you don't need to be overwhelmed by all of the information this guide provides on each of the 32 distilleries. I'm going to give you some creative ways to approach these profiles, so you can quickly and easily gather an optimal list of distilleries.

Once you achieve that list, you can then organize the distilleries by region and begin planning out your days. My suggestion is choose the best two or three pruning methods from the following list, then jot down the six region names on a piece of paper, leaving space underneath them, and add each distillery you choose to its corresponding region. Don't hesitate to notate the primary reason you want to visit, as it might help you narrow things down later.

If you are like a kid in a candy store and your list looks long, it's okay. I tend to choose up to three times more distilleries than I intend to visit. This way I can whittle my list down to the best of the best or to the ones that best fit my schedule.

Here are my favorite pruning methods for creating a short list of distilleries. Choose your final list by the following:

Distilleries You Know

Sure, this is the basic method that most people use, but it shouldn't be ignored. You don't want to miss a distillery you've been looking forward to seeing your whole life. Look through the list of distilleries and write down the ones you are most curious about.

Brands You Know

This is the most logical way to choose a distillery, but it can be difficult to know who makes which brand.

Never fear: I have included a handy brand guide in the back of this book. Scribble down your favorite brands, then find them in the alphabetical list and write down each brand's corresponding distillery. For example, if you like Rebel Yell, when you find it on the list you'll see it comes from Lux Row Distillery in Bardstown. If you like Elijah Craig, it matches up with Heaven Hill also in Bardstown. And if you are curious about Pappy Van Winkle, Buffalo Trace in Frankfort is where you'll be directed. When you compile your list, make sure to write the brand name with the distillery name, so you don't forget the connection.

But remember, just because that distillery makes a particular bourbon doesn't mean you will get to sample that exact whiskey at the end of your tour.

To help you get a sense of what you might taste during your visit, I have included what I was served on my tour in each distillery profile. Use this as a loose guide to help you get an idea of what you might be tasting.

However, bear in mind that tasting selections are added and removed all the time. The purpose of these tastings is for the distillery to entice you to buy what they want to sell. So it's most likely that your offerings will be popular bourbons or something new they want you to add to your collection. Don't expect a sample of Pappy Van Winkle at Buffalo Trace. That said, I have encountered some unexpected surprises during my tastings at some distilleries, so enjoy the surprise when it happens.

Recommendations

When I started planning my first distillery adventure, I found traveler reviews on Google Maps and TripAdvisor helpful in providing further confirmation of my choices. I will warn you though, most people love just about every distillery tour they go on, and many reviewers have only experienced one or two distilleries. So try to dig beyond the accolades for the overall tour and see if you can spot something specific that might draw you to that distillery. Also remember that each distillery has multiple tour guides with different experience levels, stories, and personalities. So don't expect to have the same guide or experience as the reviewer.

Friends and acquaintances can also be a great resource for advice. Maybe you have a friend who has recently returned from Kentucky, in which case see what distilleries they enjoyed.

If you are at your favorite pub or a whiskey festival, ask bartenders or patrons for their advice on distilleries they have visited.

Social media can also provide a wealth of feedback. Instagram, Facebook, YouTube, and Pinterest feature thousands of people who have traveled to distilleries and who would love to recommend their favorites.

One of the most overlooked sources for great distillery advice is from other tour participants. While you are enjoying a tour, talk to others about their favorite distillery visits. This can be helpful in planning out your next trip or filling in gaps in your current itinerary. And that leads me to another piece of advice. If you are in a region for two days or more, plan in flex time. During my first trip to Kentucky, there were tours I had heard such glowing remarks about that I kicked myself for not having enough extra time to fit them in.

Enhanced Experiences

I loaded the profiles in this book with tons of information on standard distillery tours, but most distilleries also offer enhanced experiences such as deeper tastings or extended tours.

For example, I love whiskey and I love chocolate. Put them together and it is heaven. While doing my planning I learned that the Evan Williams Tasting Experience on Whiskey Row in Louisville had a "Sweet and Neat" chocolate and whiskey pairing on Thursdays. This wasn't a tour, but a guided tasting. It provided an excellent break from the history and distilling lessons of standard tours.

Also keep your eye out for special events. Distilleries like Castle & Key and Jeptha Creed provide opportunities for tasting and entertainment by hosting local concerts on-site. And several distilleries provide unique holiday themed tours, ghost tours, or even the chance to see the distillery without a formal tour.

If you want to immerse yourself in a particular distillery, there may be a possibility of doing extended tastings at the end of the tour—or even to skip the tour all together and just do the tasting. Some distilleries have their own bars and cocktail lounges available at the end of the tour. Just make sure you have a designated driver or car-hire option in cases where you are having an extra taste.

If you are planning on visiting five or more distilleries on a trip, I highly recommend choosing some kind of special experience for at least one of your distillery visits. Variety is the spice of life, and it adds zest to any Kentucky distillery experience.

Perks and Keepsakes

Who said that there is no such thing as a free lunch? If you head to Buffalo Trace or Barton 1792, the free tour concludes with a complimentary tasting. Some distilleries—like Bulleit and Michter's—have added in new sensory tasting experiences that go beyond just putting a glass to your lips. Others have added chocolate pairings to their standard tastings. And quite a few distilleries will send you home with free glassware as a keepsake.

When you read the distillery profiles, you will see me mention any special keepsakes or events that I enjoyed as part of my tour. This does not guarantee you will have the same experience, as distilleries always have the option to change their special offerings, but it can give you a loose idea of what freebies and extras you might receive.

I wouldn't use this as your only factor for choosing a tour, but if you are having trouble pruning down your list then a special keepsake or perk could be all you need to tip the scale in a particular distillery's favor.

Keep in mind, the cool part of perks is that they sometimes just happen—for instance, you might find Wild Turkey's legendary master distiller Jimmy Russell joining your tour or a tour guide might sneak you some white dog right off the still.

Price

Unfortunately, almost all tours cost money and your decision on which distilleries you visit or how many you visit could come down strictly to budget. And, like everything else, tour prices are going up, which makes planning even tougher. Just between 2018 and 2020 tour prices jumped 20% or more across the board.

I wanted to place exact pricing for tours in the distillery guide, but by the time this reaches you the prices could change again. So I have added in dollar symbols to show you a range of prices.

Here's what each symbol relates to:

- Free = Free
- $ = $0.01–9
- $$ = $9–15
- $$$ = $16–24
- $$$$ = over $25

Use these figures as an estimate, then double check the current prices on the distillery's website before making your final decision. Don't forget to make reservations for the most important tours, especially if you are traveling during a busy tourist season. Tours do frequently sell out. Also note that extended tastings and special experiences will cost more.

Distillery History and Architecture

Drive along Glenns Creek south of Frankfort and see the ruins of the 19th century Old Crow Distillery, the castle that houses the Castle & Key Distillery, or the Woodford Reserve Distillery where Dr. James C. Crow perfected the sour mash process. Or enjoy the distilleries along Whiskey Row in Louisville and marvel at the revival of long-standing Richardsonian Romanesque architecture. See the historic warehouses of Buffalo Trace or the Spanish mission architecture of Four Roses. Or make your way to Old Talbott Tavern, the world's oldest bourbon bar, for a flight and a chance to sit at the same bar where the legends of Kentucky also sat. There is no shortage of history or stunning architecture around these distilleries. Even some newer distilleries like Neeley Family Distillery, James E. Pepper, and Casey Jones unveil amazing stories of yesteryear. For the history buff, the choices are endless.

Location and Region

In town for the Kentucky Derby? Been planning a trip to Cincinnati? Maybe your long lost aunt lives near Lexington. With distilleries all over Kentucky, you are likely to have a distillery near where you are visiting. Maybe you have already tried a bunch of distilleries in one area and want to experience another region of Kentucky. There are several distilleries west, east, and north of the traditional distillery region of central Kentucky: head east to historic Old Pogue, or way out west to O.Z. Tyler in Owensboro, or check in on the banks of the Ohio River at New Riff or Second Sight—both are just across the river from Cincinnati.

One of the best regions for a first-timer is in and around Louisville's Whiskey Row. Get a hotel or an Airbnb; stroll along Whiskey Row (Main Street) and enjoy distilleries, amazing food, whiskey bars, nighttime entertainment, a ballgame at Louisville Slugger Field, and visit the Louisville Slugger Museum. And as a bourbon fan, you should definitely make time to visit the third floor of the Frazier Museum. As you walk through its halls you will learn about bourbon's amazing depth of history, see a fantastic collection of bourbon bottles, and, using an amazing interactive display, learn about the brands and the characters that made bourbon what it is today.

KEEP A WISH LIST

It will be hard to see every Kentucky distillery you want to see in a single trip. Keep a list from your current research or bookmark the distilleries that will require a future visit. By using the online distillery guide and wishlist feature at **www.whiskey-lore.com/distilleries** you can make sure you don't lose track of your selections. As you try new bourbons or talk to friends about your trip, your list is going to grow. A wish list will help you be prepared for planning your next bourbon experience.

If you just can't stand it anymore, take some time to view the distilleries in the back of this book and start making your top ten or 20 list right now. When you feel you have the ultimate list of distilleries picked out, come back to this section and I will help you figure out how to arrange them, time them out, secure your tour reservations, and plan your lodging and transportation.

The Logistics of Distillery Planning

This is where it gets very real! You have committed to the trip. You have decided on all of the distilleries you would like to visit. Now it's time to create your itinerary.

HOW MANY DISTILLERIES PER DAY?

How many distilleries can you plan to visit in a single day? Well, that depends on how intense you or your companions want to be. It also depends on the tours you are doing, the region you are visiting, and the days of the week. On a normal day, it is possible to do three standard distillery tours. It would be possible to plan four tours, if they are all in a very centralized area like Whiskey Row in Louisville and one of them stays open past 5 p.m., but you may be rushing things. Remember to build in time for meals and diversions, as well as flex time so you can potentially add another distillery on the fly.

If you are traveling with others, remember that not everyone may want to tick off distilleries as quickly as you. If that is a potential concern, make sure you leave even more flex time in your schedule.

If you plan some extended tours or tastings, schedule those for the end of the day. It is hard to determine how much longer these events will run and most likely you will want to linger after the allotted time to chat with fellow travelers and enjoy an additional cocktail.

If you are heading out west, it will be difficult to fit in three or more distilleries in a single day. Keep in mind the amount of driving time between each distillery.

On Sundays, distilleries start their tours later in the morning or in early afternoon, which may prevent you from reaching three distilleries in a day. That said, there is a way to make it work. Many distilleries will open around 11 a.m. or later on Sundays; so if you are trying to fit in three distilleries that day, make sure the first one has an 11 a.m. time slot. Then, if the other two distilleries are close, plan one for 2 p.m. and another for 4 p.m. But be aware that the last tour time may be at 3 p.m. at some distilleries, in which case any early closing distilleries should be planned for the middle of the day, rather than as your last tour.

One thing I definitely want you to be aware of; in the distillery profiles, the hours listed are not hours of operations, but rather the time from the start of the first tour to the start of the last tour. So if it says 11 a.m. to 3 p.m., that means the last tour starts at 3 p.m.

Also remember that tour times are subject to change and you should only use this guide's hours as a rough planning guide—be sure to verify times on the distillery's website before solidifying your plans.

HOW MUCH TIME TO PLAN FOR EACH DISTILLERY?

It is very easy to over-schedule your day when planning distillery visits, and a loaded schedule can cause stress and frustration. Let's look at some factors you should consider when spacing out your distillery visits on your itinerary.

The first factor is tour length. When you look at the distillery profiles, you will notice that I haven't listed how long the tours are. This is because tour times can vary drastically from what may be stated.

Here is basically what you can expect: if it is suggested that a tour is 60 minutes long, this usually means the first 45 minutes will be the actual tour and the last 15 minutes will be the tasting—but not always. I have been on some tours that run for 60 minutes before the tasting. There are also distilleries like the Jim Beam American Stillhouse where the tour is actually a full 90 minutes. Make sure you get an idea of the tour length when making your reservation.

Sometimes outside factors extend the time needed to visit a distillery. If a tour guide is talkative or if guests ask a million questions, then you are headed for overtime. Or you may hit it off with fellow travelers and want to continue a fun conversation, but the pinch of a tight itinerary has you running away.

I would recommend that you should pad your distillery time with an extra 30 minutes, at the very least.

The next factor is your driving or walking time. Never assume you will get to the next location without hitting every stop light, needing to buy gasoline, or being slowed by a traffic incident. Plan your time out, but add 15 minutes or more to give yourself a cushion for unexpected travel events.

We all have to eat and on a day of having whiskey samples it is even more important to keep our bellies content. Build in a lunch break of an hour or more—and a dinner hour if you're planning an early evening tour.

The last factor you should keep in mind is that distilleries like you to check in for your tour 15 minutes ahead of its starting time. Don't push things until the last minute or you might lose your chance to tour—or, worse yet, you might hold up the other visitors.

SHOULD YOU GET RESERVATIONS?

Distillery tours are getting more and more popular. As a result, it has become much more important to consider getting reservations, especially during the busy summer season or if you are doing a limited edition tour.

One example is the Barton 1792's Estate Tour. This intimate tour only runs once a day. Because of the tour size and the fact that it is free, you will most likely miss out if you don't reserve your spot. Another example is any Buffalo Trace extended tour: these are also free and sometimes require reservations weeks or months in advance.

The simplest way to get tickets is to use the distillery's website to do so, ideally as soon as you know your plans. Don't worry, there shouldn't be anything to print: I have never had a distillery ask me for a printed ticket (just make sure you have access to your email in case they lose your reservation). In most cases, when you arrive, the distillery will just verify your reservation by name. Another option is that if you will be in an area for two or more days, stop by the distillery the day before you want to visit and attempt to secure your tickets in person.

Just be aware that there are exceptions to every rule. At the Jim Beam American Stillhouse they stop taking reservations online two days before the tour starts. You may be able to get walk-up tickets, but this does mean that you could miss out.

To save you from hunting around websites, I have added direct links to each distillery's tour reservation page in the online guide at *www.whiskey-lore.com/distilleries*.

Getting To and Around Kentucky

Once you have your rough sketch of distilleries completed, it is time to figure out how you will get to and around the state. Planes, trains, buses, and automobiles are at your disposal.

And what about the concern about drinking and driving? Yes, I will cover that too.

BY PLANE

If Kentucky is a fair distance from where you live, your best bet for reaching bourbon country is probably to hop aboard a jet. There are three primary in-state airports that provide easy access to various regions of Kentucky.

Cincinnati/Northern Kentucky International Airport (CVG)
From here you can take the 2x bus into Cincinnati in order to visit two distilleries right across the river in Covington. Alternatively, you can rent a car to easily reach north, central, and Lexington region distilleries within two hours.

Lexington Blue Grass Airport (LEX)
If you want to avoid renting a car, but still have access to several distilleries, this airport will give you easy access to the Lexington Distillery District. Look for bus #21 to get you from the airport to downtown Lexington; alternatively, a ride-share could take you there with a little less effort. If you do rent a car, the central region is a short drive to the west of the airport.

Louisville Muhammad Ali International Airport (SDF)

To head into Louisville from here, take the TARC 02 bus straight from the terminal to the downtown area. From there you can rely on ride-shares or your feet to get around. If you want to head to Bardstown, west or central Kentucky, you will need a tour agency or a rental car to reach your destination.

Other regional airports include:

Owensboro Daviess County Regional Airport (OWB)

This airport easily serves the west region. As it's a regional airport, expect a higher price for your plane ticket and the need for a rental car to reach your destination.

Paducah Barkley Regional Airport (PAH)

Another option for the west region, this regional airport will most likely require a rental car for your onward journey.

Out of state airport:

Nashville International Airport (BNA)

This airport is an option for visiting both the Bardstown and west regions, and could be a great option if you want to add Tennessee sour mash to your itinerary. However, be aware that you will need to rent a car and drive for two hours before you get to your first Kentucky distillery.

BY TRAIN

This may not seem like the modern way to travel, but Amtrak can be a great way to enjoy a nice comfortable seat while letting somebody else take you there. It is also helpful for those that don't like to fly. Since trains were critical to the growth of the bourbon industry, there is something fitting about a ride on the rails to get to bourbon country.

While there are two Amtrak routes that lead to Kentucky, both will require alternate transportation to reach car rental options.

City of New Orleans

Yes, the very one that old Arlo Guthrie rambles on about in his classic 1970s song, which is fitting as the train covers some of America's great music centers, including New Orleans and Chicago (the cities it starts/ends at), and Memphis. For those distilleries close to the Mississippi River, you can take this train to Fulton, Kentucky. However, the closest car rental location is in Mayfield, Kentucky, 20 miles northeast which may require a taxi or a ride on Greyhound.

Cardinal

This is the best option for people coming from the northeast. With its inception in New York City, the train rolls through Philadelphia, Baltimore, Washington, Charlottesville (VA), Charleston (WV), Ashland (KY), Cincinnati, Indianapolis, and on to Chicago. Overall this is the best option along the rails, but it still will require a taxi ride and rental car if you want to travel beyond the Covington area distilleries.

BY BUS

Buses provides the ultimate budget-friendly way to travel to Kentucky, and national carrier Greyhound provides various stops across the state. While you won't be able to reach most rural distilleries, including Bardstown, this can be an option for adding on Owensboro or jumping up to Cincinnati from Louisville, or even just taking a jump into Frankfort from Lexington or Louisville. A list of bus stations in Kentucky can be found here: *www.greyhound.com*

Louisville, Covington (Cincinnati), Frankfort, and Lexington offer local bus services. Check each provider's website for prices, hours, and stops.

- **Louisville:** *www.ridetarc.org*
- **LouLift (Louisville):** *(*free bus rides between distilleries)
  www.kybourbontrail.com/wp-content/uploads/2019/05/TARC_LouLift_Brochure.pdf
- **Covington:** *www.tankbus.org*
- **Frankfort:** *www.frankfort.ky.gov/216/Frankfort-Transit*
- **Lexington:** *www.lextran.com*

BY AUTOMOBILE

Love a road trip? Well, Kentucky offers some of the most beautiful blue-green grasses and rolling hills you will ever see. Most spots in the state are accessible by car.

> *Side note: The one thing to watch for are hotels that have restrictions on parking; this will generally happen in cities like Louisville and Lexington, but could also occur in areas like Bardstown. The good news is, in Bardstown at least, that there is always street parking.*

A car will provide you with the ultimate freedom. But bear in mind that very few distilleries are within walking distance of other distilleries or accommodations. This means you should expect to drive to get from point A to point B.

If you have a partner or are traveling in a group, it's always best to select a designated driver. But if there is only one person available to drive, then let's look at the issue of post tour tastings and getting safely to your next destination.

Please Drink Responsibly!

We have all heard the tragedies when people act irresponsibly by drinking and driving. You are not only endangering your own life but also the lives of your passengers and others on the road. Don't be one of those who regrets an error in judgment for the rest of their lives.

I will provide you with some guidelines for driving between distilleries—however, always use your best judgment. Remember that our bodies all handle alcohol differently, especially smaller quantities. Know your limitations, and if you are planning on drinking beyond your tour, definitely make other plans for getting from the distillery to your next destination.

Now here's an interesting fact. Kentucky's state law does not allow distilleries to serve over 1.75 ounces (50 ml) of whiskey during their standard after-tour tastings.

According to Alcohol.org, a female at 100 lbs, consuming 1.75 oz of 80 proof whiskey and entering a vehicle five minutes after drinking would measure at 0.06%. Understand that this is just an estimate and there is no guarantee your tour will stick to 80 proof samples (in fact, most don't). There are several tours where you will taste cask-strength whiskey that can rise to 120 proof or white dog that can be even higher. And, as I've said before, everyone's body handles alcohol differently. Then there's other factors such as how long it has been since you last consumed a meal that will play a part. If you are feeling tipsy, get a ride-share or a taxi.

If you want to get a rough idea of how your height and weight affect your blood alcohol level, a handy calculator can be found here: *www.alcohol.org/bac-calculator*

Even better, you can buy your own pocket breathalyzer and carry that with you. Check *www.whiskey-lore.com/shop* for some options.

> *Side note: At 80 proof, 1.75 oz (50 ml) of bourbon is comparable to a 12 oz beer at 5% alcohol.*

Carry Snacks with You

It's always good to have a bag of trail mix or some snack that you can munch on in-between tours. Time may be limited before your tour and having food in your stomach can help reduce the effect of alcohol in your system.

Sleep Near the Distillery

No, this is not suggesting you pull up some blades of grass outside the distillery to catch some z's. Instead, find a hotel or Airbnb within walking distance or a short ride-share from the distillery. That way you won't have to worry about driving, and you can safely ride or walk back to your accommodations. Rural distilleries will make this more difficult—be sure to plan not to drink extra when you have to drive to get to your next destination.

Have a Backup Plan

Sometimes you will get caught up in the moment and consume more than you should. Always have a backup plan. Knowing there are taxis, shuttle services, or ride-shares available can keep you out of a lot of trouble.

BY RIDE-SHARE

Services like Uber and Lyft are a wonderful addition to the bourbon tour landscape. With them, it's much easier to travel to a variety of distilleries and enjoy the experience without fear of driving while intoxicated.

However, at the time of writing, these services are not available in many rural areas of Kentucky—especially the western end of the state. That said, Lyft has recently made its way into Bardstown, so some areas are covered. Check your app when you are in town or ask the distillery to suggest a local taxi service.

Accommodations

There are a variety of lodging options throughout Kentucky. My advice would be to choose your accommodations based on the location of your last tour of the day.

HOTELS AND MOTELS

The most obvious of choices. Hotels and motels are scattered throughout the state and you can use your favorite Online Travel Agents (OTAs) like Hotels.com, Booking.com, Kayak, etc to find the right place to stay, or be loyal to your favorite brands and earn points by staying at their hotels.

AIRBNBS AND HOME RENTALS

Airbnbs can be an inexpensive option, and it's often much easier to find something closer to rural distilleries than with more traditional lodgings. I have found some exceptional accommodations in cities, including some historically significant ones in places like Old Louisville and Cincinnati, by searching airbnb.com. There are also other home rental options such as VRBO by HomeAway and FlipKey.

CAMPING AND RVS

The rural nature of Kentucky makes camping or taking an RV interesting options. There are a variety of parks throughout the state and you can also use websites like freecampsites.net to find great places to park. The only drawback may be if you are also planning to visit some city-based distilleries. In that case, you will need to find a ride-share option.

ON-SITE ACCOMMODATIONS

The good news is that distilleries such as Willett and Bardstown Bourbon Company are now building out on-site accommodations. The bad news is that they are not there yet. Just be patient: this will be an incredible option in the future.

Old Talbott Tavern Inn is about as close as you can get to an on-site accommodation. Located in the center of Bardstown, this historic inn is a short ride from several distilleries including Barton 1792, Willett, Bardstown Bourbon Company, Preservation, and Lux Row as well as the Heaven Hill Bourbon Heritage Center.

Side Trips

Variety is the spice of life. Don't just cling to distilleries when you are in Kentucky. There are a ton of fun places to see and explore. Maybe you are into nature, amusement parks, horse racing, or just incredible scenery and road trips. You will find all of that and more in the Bluegrass State.

To make your planning even easier, I have suggested side trips with every distillery. Just look at the end of the distillery's profile and choose your favorites from the suggestions.

Here are some examples of fun non-bourbon experiences:

- Abraham Lincoln's Boyhood Home at Knob Creek or Lincoln Homestead State Park
- Ark Encounter, a recreation of Noah's Ark
- Frazier History Museum
- Horse Farms
- Keeneland Race Course
- Kentucky Derby Museum and Churchill Downs
- Louisville Slugger Museum
- The Martha Layne Collins Bluegrass Parkway
- Sports including the Cincinnati Reds, Kentucky Wildcats, Louisville Cardinals, and Louisville Bats

If you are bringing along children or someone who isn't as into bourbon as you, you will thank me for suggesting these little bourbon breaks.

COOPERAGES

The one thing missing from every distillery tour (except for Old Forester in Louisville) is the experience of a fully functioning cooperage. Barrel making is an amazing craft and something that would make an excellent addition to your time in Kentucky.

You'll find that most of the large distilleries in Kentucky get their barrels from the Kentucky Cooperage (Independent Stave Company). Here you can see the way they gas flame barrels to meet the different char levels required by each distillery. It is right down the road from Limestone Branch and Maker's Mark distilleries; they are open Monday through Friday and tours (by reservation) cost around $10.

There are other cooperages in the state, but Kentucky Cooperage is the only one open for touring.

WHAT ABOUT BOURBON FESTIVALS?

Another great way to experience the best of Kentucky bourbon is to attend a festival. A festival enables you to go to one location where the distilleries come to you. This can be a wonderful opportunity for tasting various types of whiskey from the larger manufacturers, while also discovering new tastes from smaller craft distilleries. And because they are in one location, you won't have to worry about driving from distillery to distillery.

If you're planning to head to a festival, you'll need to plan months ahead; some sell out very quickly and lodging also fills up fast. Expect crowds.

Here are the two big bourbon festivals in Kentucky:

- **Bourbon Classic** (Louisville, KY)
  www.bourbonclassic.com
- **Bardstown Bourbon Festival** (Bardstown, KY)
  www.kybourbonfestival.com/events

The Day of Your Tour

Here is a quick list of considerations for handling the day of the tour, being a good tour guest, and preparing for the consumption of alcohol:

- Eat before you drink.
- Bring some water. These tours can include stair climbing, hills, and walks through hot facilities, so you will get thirsty quickly.
- Try to take your time when tasting. Some tastings will feel rushed. Remember, you don't have to drink all that they offer. If you don't like one, move on. However, there are some distilleries like Willett and Four Roses that only provide a single tasting glass. This means you have to finish your last sample before they pour the next. You may just have to skip one or find a place to pour it out.
- Should you buy at the distillery? If you want to dip your own bottle in red wax at Maker's Mark, then go right ahead. As for pricing inside and outside the distillery that varies from place to place. I will say that distillery exclusives are worth investing in at

the distillery. But there have been times I have been told it was exclusive and then saw it in a store. Also, be aware that some bourbon may only be available in Kentucky.

- Don't shy away from extended tasting experiences; many of them are worth the extra that you spend.
- Be prepared with questions for your guide. Nothing is more boring than a tour group that just tags along for the ride. Ask about the differences between their process and other distilleries. Find out what their mash bill is, if they don't tell you on the tour. Ask how long their fermentation process is or what their favorite whiskey is—you might find out your tour guide prefers another brand! This book should provide you with plenty of ammunition in the way of questions.
- Bring some tip money and thank guides that do an extraordinary job. I know these tours are getting more expensive, but a great tour guide who shows passion and makes your day by providing a memorable experience is worth $2 to $5 or more.

Keeping Track of Your Plans

Congratulations! You are now officially prepared to plan out the entire course of your Kentucky bourbon experience. Give yourself a little pat on the back. Then start firming up the distilleries you want to visit each day by plotting them out.

One thing that can help immensely is starting a document with each day of your trip set as a headline. I prefer Google Docs because I can always access them from my phone or laptop—just make sure to download an offline version. Then start filling in your desired tours and times under each day's heading.

Next, fill in side trips and then find your accommodations for each evening. Time out the distance between each distillery and make sure to put in enough time between to allow for driving and breaks.

I like to wait on pulling the trigger on any kind of reservation until after I have a solid plan for each day. The first thing is to make sure that you can secure the transportation you need to get to Kentucky. Then, start booking your tours by using the "Book Your Tour" links in each distillery profile. If the distillery provides one, add the confirmation number for your tour to the document. Place all of your hotel and car rental confirmations on this same document to make sure you have easy access, should you need it.

Now there is nothing left to do except prepare our palates.

PART THREE

WHISKEY TASTING PREPARATION

〜〜〜〜〜〜〜〜〜〜〜〜〜〜〜〜〜〜〜〜

"Too much of anything is bad, but too much good whiskey is barely enough."

Mark Twain, author

PART 3
Whiskey Tasting Preparation

When heading to Kentucky for a bourbon adventure, there are those that long to learn the whiskey making process, while others love the stories and distillery histories. The one thing we can all agree on is our desire to try some amazing spirits.

However, if you just head to Kentucky and start knocking back those little samples mindlessly then you will miss a great opportunity to dig deeper into what makes each of these bourbons unique.

While each distillery will have its own way of telling you how to enjoy their whiskey, it's worth knowing that all distilleries will pour your bourbon straight from the bottle, with nothing added to dilute it. For the uninitiated, this can lead to a sensory overload and a lost opportunity to reveal the deeper character of the whiskey. This is how tastings become more about experiential characteristics like smooth, harsh, or intense, rather than about the flavor profile. If you are used to wine tastings, whiskey is going to be a lot more in your face.

So rather than having you throw away these valuable tasting opportunities, the following pages will give you preparation tips and strategies to help you take full advantage of your bourbon experience. This way you can be more present during your initial tastings and make more informed decisions on which bourbons to buy and recommend to friends.

TO ICE OR NOT TO ICE
The way you drink bourbon is a personal choice. Here are the ways you can get the most out of the spirit.

In Cocktails and as Mixers
Whether it be a Mint Julep at the Kentucky Derby, a Jim Beam and ginger ale at home, or a Manhattan or an Old Fashioned at the bar, cocktails are a creative and flavorful way to enjoy a bourbon.

On the Rocks
For those that love the taste of bourbon and want to cool down on a hot summer's day, adding two or three ice cubes to your whiskey will do nicely. Adding ice is also a good way to introduce yourself to the taste of bourbon without overloading the senses.

Neat
If you want to enjoy a bourbon the way the master distiller envisioned it, then order it neat. Some people find this the hardcore way to enjoy a bourbon, but an unadulterated pour provides a greater chance to discover mouthfeel and delicate undertones that are masked when adding ice or cocktail ingredients.

With a Splash

While neat has its place, a splash of water in bourbon can reveal a whole new sensory experience. The more oils a bourbon contains, the more water can break that up and unveil hidden flavors and aromas that are just waiting for a chance to surface.

As most Kentucky distillers and tour guides will tell you, it is your bourbon so enjoy it however you like it. I agree with that sentiment, mostly. But if you are planning on using a 23 year old Pappy Van Winkle in a cocktail, that might be a bit pricey for something you are going to dilute. Still, if you have money to burn or you feel that that particular bourbon is the only way you can achieve the perfect cocktail, go for it.

Just remember, when you go to a distillery for a tasting, neat or with a splash will likely be your only two options. I would say that 95% of the distilleries handle bourbon tastings this way.

And this is the very reason, I want to use this opportunity to help you prepare your palate for a stronger spirit.

But before you head over to grab a bottle of bourbon, let's make sure we have the right tool for the job.

THE DRINKING GLASS

Just like a scientist or doctor, you will need the right equipment to create a consistent environment to do a proper tasting. For the bourbon enthusiast, this will be the drinking glass.

To me, the tumbler (AKA the rocks glass, old fashioned glass, or lowball glass) is the perfect vessel for whiskey on the rocks.

But for bourbon tasting tours, most distilleries use a Glencairn whiskey glass. Created by Glencairn Crystal Studio Ltd. in Scotland, these glasses were developed as a sturdy replacement for the stemmed tulip or copita glasses traditionally used by master distillers. Since their introduction to the market in 2001, full-sized and miniature Glencairn glasses have quickly become the industry standard for distillery tastings.

I would highly recommend purchasing one or two of these glasses to do your practice tastings at home. The advantage of this glass is that it concentrates the vapors of the bourbon on the nose, giving you a better chance of picking up specific aromas during a tasting. As you will learn in a moment, smelling whiskey is a major part of the tasting experience.

These glasses sell from anywhere between $5 and $20 each; you can find them in specialty shops, online, or at **www.whiskey-lore.com/shop**. And check the keepsake sections from the profiles later in this guide because there is also a good chance that you will get a free glass during your tours.

Now that you have some bourbon and your Glencairn whiskey glass, it is time to learn how to approach the aromas and taste of your whiskey.

Pour some bourbon into your Glencairn glass. This is not a drinking contest. You should only put enough whiskey in the glass to draw out two to three tastes. Remember, on the tours they can't give you more than a single shot for the entire tasting, even if you sample five whiskeys, so get used to having about ten to 20 millilitres (or a quarter to a fifth of an ounce) of bourbon in your glass. Keep in mind that we are here to discover the whiskey, not drown ourselves in it.

> **Side note:** *If you are sampling an aged bourbon, a little-known secret is to let the bourbon rest for one minute for every year it was in the barrel. They age most bourbons between three to eight years, so letting the bourbon sit for a few minutes before drinking it will give the spirit plenty of time to settle in your glass. Whiskey experts suggest that spirits evolve as they breathe: the more refined your palate becomes, the more you will be able to experience these subtle changes in your bourbon.*

Start by picking your glass up by the base, not the bowl. Often you will see people hand warming their whiskey by cradling the bowl. In the world of cognac, the theory is that heat releases aromas in the spirit. While you may be able to argue the same for whiskey, the goal here is to standardize the environment. You won't have time at the distillery to warm your bourbon, so to be able to have an apples to apples comparison, keep the whiskey at room temperature. Save the experimentation for when you are enjoying a more substantial sample while sitting around with friends. This warming concept can make for an interesting discussion.

Raise the glass to your nose. Place your nostrils near the lower edge of the glass, inside the bowl. The glass should not be touching your face, but should be within a half inch. Open your mouth slightly and breath in lightly with both your nose and your mouth. Vapors from the bourbon enter your mouth and interact with your taste buds, adding to the nosing experience. Take in an easy breath at first. If you forcefully take in a whiff of the bourbon, you will burn your nostrils with the alcohol vapors. Smelling and tasting require patience and focus.

So what did you smell? If you just said bourbon, that is okay. It takes time and experience to discover specific scents and the smells you will find initially are usually the ones you're most familiar with. For instance, if you love green apples, that might be the first scent that jumps out at you. But you may think you can't smell anything at all.

Don't overwhelm yourself. Start by trying to identify a single scent. Two smells most commonly associated with bourbon are vanilla and caramel. See if you can spot either one.

If not, no worries. It took me almost a year before I finally smelled vanilla in bourbon. Now that I have made that connection, I smell it all the time.

Don't drink yet. Take the glass away from your nose and swirl the whiskey around the base of the glass. Watch as liquid clings to the inside of the glass. We refer to these oily strands as the legs of a whiskey. The legs can give you a visual representation of the mouthfeel that you can expect (I'll define mouthfeel in a moment). The faster the legs stream down the glass, the lighter the mouthfeel of the whiskey. Roll the bourbon around the glass to view the legs and to wake it up. After rolling it, give the bourbon another nosing to see if the aromas intensify or if it uncovers something new.

Also note the color of the whiskey. The longer a bourbon remains in a barrel, interacting with the wood, the darker its color. It can also be affected by higher proofs or additional aging in finishing barrels that were previously filled with another spirit like sherry or port wine.

Now for the tasting. Bring the glass up to your face. Breathe in lightly through your nose and mouth as the bourbon slowly reaches your lips. Remember, your nose and mouth will work together to give you the full flavor experience. Put just enough whiskey on your tongue to coat it. This first sip is not where we start analyzing and seeking out flavor notes; this is an attempt to shock your tongue to prepare it for the tasting. Alcohol is an unnatural element that takes some getting used to. It might be slightly unpleasant for a moment. But just think of it as a little pain before pleasure.

Now we are ready for the official taste. But before you sip, let me explain where to focus your attention as you start your analysis.

Nosing

Now that you have had your initial intake of whiskey, see how the nose (smell) evolves from your first experience with it? Sometimes this second approach will reveal new aromas. Remember to breathe in with your mouth and nose while the liquid prepares to enter your mouth.

The Palate

Try to put into words the flavors and sensations you experience when the whiskey first hits your tongue. Do any flavors jump out at you? Is there a heavy alcohol bite or was it a smoother experience? Does the initial flavor have an impact or is it subtle or non-existent?

The Mouthfeel

To me, this is one of the most interesting and underappreciated variables in the tasting experience. It is part of the reason I have ditched the habit of putting ice in my bourbon. Each whiskey has a certain viscosity. A heavy whiskey, rich in oils, will lay heavy and thick upon the tongue, creating a silky or milky feeling. By contrast, a thinner bourbon will wash away quickly, leaving a less impressive experience. The mouthfeel doesn't necessarily suggest a higher or lower quality bourbon, but depending on your personal preference, it could be a reason you choose one bourbon over another.

An interesting byproduct of determining mouthfeel is that you will start noticing it in other liquids. Even different waters can feel lighter or heavier on the tongue.

The Finish

Think of this as the bourbon's aftertaste.

Bourbon will usually have a burn as it goes down the throat. With the assistance of Booker Noe (sixth generation master distiller from Jim Beam), this burn now has an unofficial name—the Kentucky Hug.

Don't make the mistake of assuming the hug is somehow a defect in the whiskey. The corn in the mash bill is most responsible for this burn, so with all bourbons being 51% (or more) corn, it's difficult to avoid.

And some people look forward to the hug as part of the bourbon tasting event. They suggest it warms you up. It's all in how you label it.

If you want to tame the hug, try holding the whiskey in your mouth a little longer. This dilutes the whiskey and allows it to go down easier. Of course, more time on the tongue may lead to a Kentucky Tongue instead of a Kentucky Hug.

You should also try to sense which flavors stick and which disappear quickly during the finish. Some whiskeys have a long finish and others a short finish. It is all part of the tasting experience and each person appreciates different variables.

Side note: The term smooth has become a convenient crutch for inexperienced tasters. To quickly develop your palate, start looking deeper and determining what it is about the bourbon that gives you the impression that it is smooth. Is there less of a Kentucky Hug? Does the bourbon have a well rounded experience from palate to finish? Or does it have a nice silky mouthfeel? The more you dig beyond generic terms, the sooner you will be seen as a bourbon aficionado.

THE TASTING BEGINS

Okay, it is time for the analysis. Bring the bourbon back up to your lips and this time take a more substantial amount of alcohol into your mouth. You should experience much less burn than you did the first time and the initial flavors should be more prominent on your tongue.

Get your mouth fully engaged with the whiskey. There are several methods for doing this. Here, Booker Noe strikes again. He suggested using a chewing motion to get the bourbon agitated and distributed around the mouth; a bit like a cow chewing its cud. He termed it the Kentucky Chew. It might look a little embarrassing, but remember that you will not be the only one at a Kentucky distillery using this technique.

Don't get carried away. I have seen some people treating their whiskey like mouthwash, making aggressive charges with it around their teeth and sloshing it from cheek-to cheek. This is probably excessive. There is no evidence that your teeth taste whiskey.

I prefer a slightly more subtle way of doing the Kentucky Chew. I focus on the top of the tongue and then work the whiskey around the front and sides of my mouth.

On the top of your tongue, you get a true sense of the mouthfeel. Sit with it there for a couple moments. Then, as you roll it to the sides of your tongue, you will notice other flavors and sensations unveiling themselves.

There is a myth about how we have taste sectors on our tongues with sour, sweet, bitter, umami, and salty taste buds located in specific areas. Unfortunately, this isn't true. That said, various flavors do tend to have more impact on certain areas of the tongue; and everybody's tongue has different sensitivities in different areas. I tend to get spicy flavors on the sides of my tongue.

Also, as you move whiskey around your mouth, vapors actually travel to the back of your mouth and up through your nasopharynx into your nose. In other words, even with your mouth closed, your nose is still helping you determine flavor profiles. This is why whiskey can taste flat if you have a stuffy nose. You also have taste buds on the roof of your mouth and down your throat. See how flavors change as you move whiskey around your mouth and after you swallow it. If you want to hear more about how we taste, check out the Whiskey Lore Season Two episode called *Tongue Map and How We Taste Whisky*.

The tour tasting is an excellent opportunity for you to share your flavor experiences and compare with others. But remember, the sensations aren't always the same for everybody, so don't feel like you are wrong if you are experiencing something that no one else does—or if others are catching things that you aren't.

I once said I detected a hint of minty toothpaste in Maker's Mark. I have never seen that on anyone else's flavor notes. It doesn't mean I'm wrong, it just means I'm coming at it with a different tongue and a different tasting history.

How long should you hold the bourbon in your mouth? Well, some bourbons will scream at you, "swallow me!" But other bourbons will be pleasant and you won't want to let them go. When you are trying to keep that bourbon in your mouth, your saliva will dilute it while you are attempting to savor it, which may make it easier to hold on to for a while. I would suggest that ten seconds might be enough for you to pick out the most pronounced flavors. But if it takes 20 seconds, then stick with it.

If you are doing the tasting at home, this is where you can have a larger sample size and sit and enjoy sip after sip, to get the full story. I have several whiskeys in my collection that seem to unveil something new every time I drink them. For me, these complex, multi-dimensional whiskeys are like new lands waiting to be explored.

As you swallow the bourbon, pay attention to the burn factor and how long the flavor lasts in your mouth. This is what they call "the finish." These are all the different factors a professional taster will focus on. And what it will show you is that bourbon is more than just a beverage, it is a heavily nuanced experience.

For your third and final taste, go through the same process. If you like, add a couple of drops of water before sampling to see if that changes the experience and opens up any other flavors you might have missed.

TAKE NOTES

A great way to speed your education on bourbon is to write down tasting notes. Get a little booklet or set up an online document where you can keep track of:

- The name of the bourbon
- The date you drank it
- The amount of water added
- What you smelled on the nose
- The flavor on your palate
- The mouthfeel
- The finish (Was there a Kentucky Hug? If so, how severe? Did any flavors linger?)
- The overall impression

Then, next time you try the same bourbon, ignore your notes and start a fresh set.

What you will find is that as your palate becomes more trained, you will pick out new flavors and begin to understand what you find pleasing and off-putting in each bourbon. You will also feel encouraged as you see the progress in your ability to pull out flavors and aromas. My ability to taste has made an incredible transformation since my first distillery tour.

Taking notes will enhance the growth of your knowledge and it will give you more confidence in tasting and talking about what makes a specific bourbon the right choice for you.

THERE IS NO NEED TO BE OVERWHELMED

When I started my bourbon journey, I had plenty of doubts about my ability to taste whiskey. It was part of the reason I went to 19 distilleries on my first trip to bourbon country.

I wanted a crash course so that I stopped sounding like a whiskey newbie. And that trip was an incredible learning opportunity.

Here are the two major lessons I learned during that trip:

Tasting is a Skill

Imagine that you want to be a great actor or athlete. Do you think you can walk onto the field and instantly compete? No. Even those born with natural abilities still need to learn how to harness their powers. There are no overnight successes. Everyone pays their dues. Some just get there faster than others. And some achieve their goals through sheer will.

Tasting whiskey is no different. No one gets it the first time they try it. It takes time to learn how to do it properly and it takes time to build experience with different flavors and styles.

If you love to cook or are a foodie, you may have a jump on the rest of us, but it will still take time to learn the unique flavors and aromas of whiskey.

The goal of your first trip should not be to come back a master, but to gain your first steps toward mastery. Bourbon is a journey—and the journey is good. Make sure you enjoy it.

Smelling and Tasting are Specific to the Individual

Reading other people's tasting notes or hearing them from a tour guide or friend can be helpful for a beginner trying to get a handle on some basic flavors and scents present in bourbon. But tasting notes are training wheels and eventually you need to trust yourself. There are no wrong answers when it comes to your tasting experience. If you taste it, then it exists for you. If someone else doesn't taste the same thing, so be it.

USING OTHER PEOPLE'S TASTING NOTES

The Power of Suggestion

Be careful of continuous use of other people's tasting notes as a crutch. If I tell you something tastes like licorice or green apples, the power of suggestion may force you into finding those two flavor notes. Your brain will zero in on what you want it to find. And you may end up missing something no one else would have caught.

As you start to grow your tasting skills, relying too heavily on someone else's tasting notes can stunt your growth and limit your experience. Start by creating your own notes first, then if you choose, use another person's review to compare and contrast with your own experiences.

Reading other people's tasting notes can be extremely valuable to your growth, so I am not suggesting to ignore them completely. But reserve accessing them until after you have established your initial relationship with a bourbon. Don't let them be the final word on what your tasting experience should be.

If I listened to others entirely, I might never have found a passion for certain bourbons. My own reasons for enjoying a bourbon are the things that will keep me coming back to it—not someone else's opinion.

Use the Experience You Have

Consider this: I can tell you something tastes like elderberry, but what if you have never had elderberry? How can you relate to my reference? And how will you ever find it in a bourbon?

We are all exposed to different foods and experiences in our lives. No two people are exactly the same.

For instance, I haven't spent my life around individual baking spices, so if you told me something smells like allspice I wouldn't know what you mean, so there would be no way that I could pick it out in a whiskey.

However, the first time I heard someone suggest allspice in a nosing, I went out and bought the spice, and took a sniff for myself. To my nose and experience, it reminded me of Russian tea. So now, when I smell certain whiskeys, if I smell Russian tea I realize I'm smelling allspice.

Remember when I said I tasted toothpaste in Maker's Mark? After breaking it down in my mind, I realized the bite of the bourbon along with a hint of mint was giving me a sensation similar to toothpaste. So my tasting notes changed from mint toothpaste to a hint of mint along with a spicy bite to the whiskey.

So relax and know that all good things come with time and experience. And don't be afraid to rattle off some bizarre tasting notes. You never know where they might lead.

Side note: The more you learn about tasting bourbon, the less important star ratings and grading scales become. You will soon discover that what is a five-star bourbon to one person is a two-star bourbon to someone else. I have heard it said there are no bad bourbons. I don't know if that's necessarily true, but I will say that beauty is in the eye of the beholder. View online and store ratings with a skeptical eye and make sure to read the flavor notes and comments instead. At least that way, you can get a feel for what people like or dislike specifically about the whiskey.

THE ART OF DISCOVERING FLAVORS AND SCENTS

So how can you simplify finding flavors and aromas on your own? I find that starting with one or two flavors is the best way. For me, apples and peanuts seem to be the easiest to discover. If vanilla and caramel are easiest for you, then you are in luck, since those are the two primary flavors and scents in bourbon. Seeking out one or two smells or tastes initially will keep you from sensory overload. And don't freak out if the scents or tastes don't come to you immediately. When you find one, write it in your notes. Next time you try the same bourbon, dig a little deeper.

I was so bad at finding vanilla that it was almost a year before I finally discovered it in a bourbon. I didn't have a good frame of reference. Was I smelling vanilla-scented candles, vanilla extract, or what? Vanilla is surprisingly diverse.

Then one day I put a glass of Henry McKenna Single Barrel Bourbon to my nose while I was thinking about vanilla extract and suddenly it hit me in the face. Now I can smell vanilla extract more clearly in other bourbons.

I equate it to that moment when you buy a certain model car and then suddenly see that model everywhere. I had to connect my senses to a frame of reference.

Some connections are tougher than others. If someone says cinnamon, are they talking about a Fireball candy or a baking spice? When you create your tasting notes, try to be that specific.

Side note: So who is adding all of these flavors to your bourbon? That is just it, no one is—at least not in the way you would normally think. These scents and flavors occur naturally through the combination of grains, distillation, and the influence of maturation in a charred oak cask. For instance, the vanilla comes from the vanillin found in the oak. Charring and barrel influence help bring this flavor note to the bourbon. Or, fruitiness can be increased by allowing longer fermentation times. Pepper and spice can come from an increase in the rye content of the mash bill. Every part of the distillery can have an influence on the flavor.

THE FLAVOR WHEEL

Something that can greatly assist your tasting and smelling progress is a flavor wheel. These handy little guides can be a big help to the beginner who has no idea where to start with finding flavors and scents.

Here are some of the combinations normally found on a bourbon flavor wheel:

Spices
These fall into two categories: brown spices (cinnamon, allspice, pepper, clove, tobacco) and savory spices (anise or liquorice, mint, herbal).

Fruit
These will include apple, tropical fruit, dried fruit, cherry, pear, peach, and berries.

Floral
Honeysuckle and rose petal

Grain
You may sense the original grains like rye, barley, or corn. Additional grains may also show through.

Sweet Aromatics
Vanilla, caramel, butterscotch, maple syrup, honey, and chocolate

Wood and Nuts
Oak, walnut, pecan, almond, peanut, and hazelnut

To get your own copy of a flavor wheel, log into *www.whiskey-lore.com/flavorwheel*.

WHO JUDGES QUALITY? YOU DO!

One of the best parts about learning to taste and smell bourbon is no longer being beholden to other's opinions of what makes a quality spirit. After a few distilleries in Kentucky and some experimentation at home, you will have the confidence you need to judge what you feel is a quality bourbon and what you would rather pass on.

Here are some things I learned by developing my palate:

Age Ain't Nothin' but a Number
It is amazing how many people get sucked in by age statements. But there are several important factors that can influence the quality of a whiskey that rests for a long time in a barrel.

In Scotland, where ten years is an average starting point for a whisky, the weather doesn't change much from season to season, so the barrel is slow to impart its influence. By contrast, the Bluegrass State is notorious for its wild weather fluctuations, so whiskey ages and evaporates much faster there. The more it evaporates, the more influence the barrel has on its flavor.

So, if you are a fan of the oak influence, and you like a nuttiness in your whiskey, then an older bourbon might be perfect for you. But if you like the fruit and other flavors that come from the original white dog, then six to eight years might be more of a sweet spot.

There are other variables that can influence how well a bourbon ages. I find that wheat forward bourbons seem to thrive more with age, whereas the spice of rye seems to diminish with too much age. Also, the placement in a warehouse and the size of the barrel can have a huge effect on the aging process.

Don't fall into the trap that older is better. It is just different.

Price Ain't Nothin' but a Number
Everybody seems to buzz about the four-figure sales numbers for a bottle of Pappy Van Winkle. If you want the whiskey as a collectable, maybe it is worth four figures to you.

But how does Pappy Van Winkle taste? Is it the absolute best whiskey for your individual palate? Or are you just buying it for status or because someone said it was good?

I am picking on Pappy because it is one of the most sought-after bottles on the market—and yet probably 90% of the people who want it have never tried it before.

Educate yourself. Sample it if you get a chance, but there is no need to buy a bottle just because it has an elevated price. If a bottle of $14 J.T.S. Brown Bottled-in-Bond does it for you, use the thousands of dollars you saved and start a college fund for your child. Or take a trip to Scotland, Ireland, or Japan to see how the rest of the world makes whisky.

SUPPLEMENT YOUR LEARNING

If you are struggling early on, it is fine to check out some YouTube videos where people do tastings and product comparisons. You will see what whiskeys others have a passion for and you will be exposed to some common threads in tasting notes.

Go to *www.whiskey-lore.com/influencers* to see my latest list of whiskey tasters and groups from around the world. And also, see some of my own tasting videos at *www.whiskey-lore.com/tasting*.

AFTER YOUR KENTUCKY EXPERIENCE

Another great way to learn is to hold a whiskey tasting party. Get three or four close friends, ask each to bring three bottles of whiskey—a higher priced, a mid-priced, and a quality bottom-shelf bargain. That'll give you nine to 12 whiskeys to taste. Sit around and discuss each one. Notice how the power of suggestion makes its way around the room. Each person will pick out their own flavors and suddenly you will detect those same flavors and experiences yourself.

Try to introduce your friends to some whiskeys you are curious about but haven't tried yet. I used to always try to sneak in a Canadian whisky or blended scotch just to see if anyone would bite.

Here are some other great ways to share your love of bourbon:

Food Pairings
Once you have done a chocolate and whiskey pairing, it is hard to shake the temptation to experiment further. Find some fun combinations and host a chocolate and whiskey pairing event of your own. Or find some great food pairings and host a guided whiskey and food pairing dinner party.

To gather some pairing ideas, head to *www.whiskey-lore.com/pairings*.

Local Events
There are plenty of whiskey tasting festivals circling the United States and across the globe. Do a quick Google search for "whiskey festivals" and see if you can find something happening in your area. Also check out local pubs and restaurants that host whiskey tasting events.

Meetup
Find whiskey fans in the area with services like *www.meetup.com* or start your own.

Find Local and Regional Distilleries
As you now know, bourbon comes from all over the United States. Don't let the fact the distillery is in Colorado, Texas, or Illinois dissuade you—the same tasting techniques apply, so go see what your local craft distillery has come up with.

Plan Your Next Adventure
Make another trip back to Kentucky or maybe expand into Tennessee whiskey. Or really expand your horizons and plan a trip to Canada, Scotland, Ireland, or even Japan.

Bourbon can create a lifetime of experiences. Let me be the first to welcome you to this wonderful world of "America's Native Spirit". If you haven't done so already, it's time to jump into the profiles and start picking out the distilleries that will make your Kentucky bourbon experience unforgettable.

PART FOUR

PROFILES: YOUR GUIDE TO KENTUCKY DISTILLERIES

Profiles: Your Guide To Kentucky Distilleries

When planning a great adventure, having tons of information at your fingertips can make all the difference in how easily your journey comes together. But if the information you collected is in various formats and varying degrees of quality it can bog you down.

When I started putting together my Kentucky adventure, I read through articles and blog posts, looked at bottles in the liquor store, read about bourbon tours on review websites, and asked anybody I could for advice. Most of the time the information was limited or scattered.

I created this guide so that you could quickly get to the heart of what each distillery is known for. I also wanted to provide a fast and easy reference guide so you could easily plan out each day's adventure without having to do a lot of website hopping.

I hope you find this guide invaluable. And if you do, please help spread the word by leaving a review on Amazon or by sharing how helpful it was on social media, and with your friends and family. Your reviews and support will help Whiskey Lore grow into a resource for whiskey travel and history all over the world.

HOW TO USE THIS GUIDE

Below, you will find profiles for 32 different Kentucky distilleries. I have visited every one of them. What I am providing is a mix of reference information and my personal experience. This is not meant to be a quality review of the distilleries. Instead it's a guide that gives you the valuable information you need for determining which distilleries fit your personality and what to expect when you visit.

You don't have to read this guide from beginning to end. Skip around to the distilleries that catch your eye. And if you have trouble finding the brands you are interested in, look in the back of the book to find a handy brand-to-distillery cross-reference.

Each profile is two pages long. Here is what you will find contained in each:

ABOUT

This part of the profile features information about the facility, the distillery's history, and basic details about the tour. This is not comprehensive: I wrote these to give you an initial impression of the distillery. My job is to get you interested in finding the ideal experience. If you want more of a history or marketing focus, check out the distillery's website.

LISTEN/WATCH FOR

Every distillery tour has something that makes it unique. I wanted to give you a chance to keep an eye out for these cool features or stories when you visit. Like going on a treasure hunt, this feature will give you something to seek out that others might miss.

2020 TASTING EXPERIENCE/KEEPSAKES*

It's important to stress here that the * signifies that your results may vary. I wanted to provide you with a list of the items I tasted during my tour and the keepsake(s) the distillery provided as gifts. Distilleries will occasionally change their offerings, especially the bourbons served during the tastings. Use this area as a loose planning point, but do not be disappointed if keepsakes or tastes are no longer offered.

GETTING THERE

Using GPS is your best bet for directions. But in this section I give some tips on parking and special considerations when heading to the distillery.

TOUR SCHEDULE

One of the most frustrating parts of using distillery websites for planning is constant age verification while trying to figure out tour times. I would have given anything to just flip back and forth between pages to get general tour times.

I have done my best to provide you with a window into each distillery's standard tour schedule. Understand that tour times can change and this is just a guide to give you a framework. Always confirm details on the distillery website when you have narrowed your list down.

Note that my hours focus on tour start times, so if the time is 10 a.m. to 3 p.m. that means the last tour leaves at 3 p.m., not that the distillery closes at that time. I also mention if the tours go on the hour, half hour, or randomly; know that this can change as well. Also be aware that certain distilleries shut down for summer or periodically throughout the year for cleaning and other reasons. Always use the distillery website for final verification before you visit.

SIDE TRIPS

We cannot live by bourbon alone. Each distillery profile features one or two diversions that will help you see more of Kentucky than just the inside of a tasting room. Your traveling companions will thank you.

CLOSEST DISTILLERIES

For each distillery I provide two further distillery suggestions that are in close range to the one being profiled. This can save a lot of plotting out on maps during your initial search.

AT A GLANCE INFORMATION

I wanted you to have important information at a glance. Besides distillery information, you will also find basic details based on the standard tour experience.

The information provided in this section includes:

Featured Brands

This is a list of popular bourbons at that distillery, as well as some wheated and rye whiskeys you'll find there. It doesn't mean they are fully produced at the distillery or that they will be available to sample; this is just to give you a sense of what brands are associated with that distillery. And this is by no means a comprehensive list.

Owner

Some distilleries are local, family-owned distilleries, and others are owned by larger parent corporations. This can give you a sense of the resources behind the distillery.

Region

This will help you to find a group of distilleries you can visit in a single day. You should be able to plan at least three distilleries a day in a single region. The regions I determined are as follows:

- Bardstown
- Central
- Lexington
- Louisville
- North
- West

Available to Tour

Each distillery features different parts of the process in their tours. If you love smelling the angel's share like I do, then make sure the distillery features "warehouse" as an option. The areas of the distillery I highlight include:

- Milling
- Lab
- Fermenters
- Column Still, Pot Still, Hybrid Still
- Warehouse
- Bottling
- Cooperage

Understand that extended tours are available at many distilleries, and they may include areas of the distillery not shown here. These are all based on the standard tour.

Cost

Distillery tour prices are subject to change, so rather than giving specific prices I have used a symbol (free–$$$$) to signify a price range. See Part 2 (Making Your Final List) for the corresponding prices for each symbol.

Location

This is the street address for the distillery and where you need to head for the tour; I've checked all addresses on Google Maps, and they should work fine with most (if not all) GPS systems.

Website

This is a link to the home page of the distillery's website.

DREW'S TOP THREE REASONS TO VISIT

This is as close to as you will get to a review. I wanted you to have a sense of the things I thought set this distillery tour apart from the others. If you are having a hard time choosing between two distilleries, this information can help you tip the scales in the right direction.

MORE INFORMATION

Books are handy for flipping through, but websites can provide some amazing organizational features and fast access links.

To get the most out of planning, make sure you have signed up for a Whiskey Lore Society membership. Head to *www.whiskey-lore.com/signup* and use the Promo Code **bourbon1792** to unlock full access to the links I provide.

Membership will allow access to all 32 distillery profiles online, including these tools:

- A **Wish List** feature that allows you to collect your favorite distilleries on your own personal Member Profile page.
- Links to the profiles of the **Closest Distilleries**.
- Map links so you can pin your favorite distilleries.
- Direct **Book a Tour** links that save you from jumping around the website.
- All of the profiles in this book and any additional Kentucky distilleries I visit in the future.

Don't miss out on this valuable tool.

While making your list, I would encourage you to stretch yourself like I did. Mix and match between large and small distilleries. I found some excellent tours at distilleries I had never heard of. The big guys may be more polished, but the little guys can show you entrepreneurial spirit and innovation.

Have fun looking through these profiles. Kentucky bourbon is right at your fingertips.

Angel's Envy Distillery

ABOUT ANGEL'S ENVY

Opened in 2013, Angel's Envy is the brainchild of long-time Brown-Forman Master Distiller and Bourbon Hall-of-Famer Lincoln Henderson who, along with his son Wes and a third generation of Hendersons, has created a unique expression in the world of bourbon. They add additional flavor notes to their four- to six-year-old bourbon by finishing it in ruby port barrels.

For visitors to downtown Louisville, the distillery is located on the eastern end of historic Whiskey Row (Main Street). It sits in a remodeled brick warehouse, where everything feels upscale from the moment you walk into the visitor's center and gift shop.

The tour starts with a complementary biodegradable box of water and an elevator ride up into the heart of the distillery. As you arrive on the second floor, the bourbon-making process will unfold before your eyes, from grain to bottle. At the tour's conclusion, you will head to the third floor for a guided tasting and chocolate pairing.

LISTEN/WATCH FOR

See how they pay homage to two former residents of the building, both the Vermont American Corporation and the original 1902 resident, the American Freight Elevator company. There are white beams with rollers in the main distilling area that were part of the elevator factory.

2020 TASTING EXPERIENCE/KEEPSAKES*

The tasting room is beautiful and the finished log table is an elegant yet rustic touch. Our sample was Angel's Envy's Kentucky Straight Bourbon with a ruby port finish, served neat in a Glencairn whiskey glass. After tasting it neat, we had a piece of ice added so we could note any difference. They also gave us a nice chocolate for pairing. Everything was served on a placemat that featured the tasting notes. There were no keepsakes.

GETTING THERE

It is a short walk to Angel's Envy from downtown Louisville. With Louisville Slugger Field across the street, there are also several parking lots available around the distillery for as low as $7 per day. Angel's Envy is a good starting point for a stroll to several downtown distilleries.

TOUR SCHEDULE

10 a.m.–4 p.m. Mon, Wed & Thu;
10 a.m.–5 p.m. Fri & Sat;
12:30–4:30 p.m. Sun
Various tours are available.

SIDE TRIPS

- **Louisville Slugger Field** - The home of the St. Louis Cardinals minor league baseball club.
- **Vendome Copper and Brass Works** No public entry. See where Kentucky's stills are manufactured.

CLOSEST DISTILLERIES

- **Rabbit Hole** (SE-0.3 miles)
- **Old Forester** (W-0.7 miles)

At A Glance

FEATURED BRANDS	Angel's Envy
OWNER	Bacardi
REGION	Louisville
AVAILABLE TO TOUR	Fermenters, Column Stills, Warehouse, Bottling
COST	$$$ - Call for military discount
LOCATION	500 E. Main St., Louisville, KY 40202
WEBSITE	*www.angelsenvy.com*

Drew's Top Three Reasons to Visit

1 The building is beautifully restored. This once abandoned elevator and tool factory features an open floor plan that demonstrates almost the entire bourbon making process just by doing a 360.

2 When you visit, you will see their barrel room loaded to the ceiling with a large variety of finishing barrels, including rum casks that finish off their Angel's Envy rye whiskey.

3 Lincoln Henderson's story is fascinating as his 39 years at Brown-Forman yielded some iconic brands including Gentleman Jack and Woodford Reserve.

MORE INFORMATION: *www.whiskey-lore.com/angelsenvy*

Bardstown Bourbon Company

ABOUT BARDSTOWN BOURBON COMPANY

Bardstown Bourbon Company may be a new name, but it is already making a major impact in the bourbon industry. Beyond their own brands, they produce spirits for a wide variety of startups and legacy labels like Jefferson's, High West, and Chicken Cock. Their unique Collaborative Distilling Program sees them producing over 40 unique mash bills.

But this is more than just a distillery. Even before it opened it was a hot spot for locals looking for a tasty lunch and delicious whiskey or cocktail from their fully stocked bar. As the facility grows, its aim is to build a Napa Valley type experience including an on-site hotel.

This is one of the few distilleries where you start and end your tour with a tasting. This is a chance to try whiskey from white dog to finished product. After your guided tasting, you enter a state of the art distillery featuring computerized systems that follow each of the 40 mash bills throughout their creation. You will see everything from where they receive the grain, through the distillation process, to an aging warehouse.

LISTEN/WATCH FOR

Are you curious to know the full range of brands they produce? When you reach the end of the tour, check out the brands they sell in the gift shop. Some may surprise you.

2020 TASTING EXPERIENCE/KEEPSAKES*

Part of the tasting took place in the classroom at the visitor's center. We had three samples, all at 120 proof: a rye whiskey distillate (white dog), a wheated bourbon maturate at two years, and a rye-bourbon maturate at two years. We also tried the Bardstown Bourbon Fusion Series #1. While in the warehouse, they gave us the opportunity to taste whiskey drawn straight from the barrel. We also received a very nice square branded tumbler, perfect for whiskey on the rocks.

GETTING THERE

If you are visiting Bardstown, you will find Bardstown Bourbon Company just south of the Kentucky Bluegrass Parkway, off of Exit 25. There is a frontage road called Parkway Drive that leads to the distillery entrance. There is ample on-site parking.

TOUR SCHEDULE

10 a.m.–4 p.m. Tue–Sun
Various tours are available.

SIDE TRIPS

- **My Old Kentucky Home** - The former home of "The Father of American Music" Stephen Foster.
- **Wickland** - The home of three Kentucky governors and one distiller.

CLOSEST DISTILLERIES

- **Lux Row** (W-2.9 miles)
- **Heaven Hill Bourbon Heritage Center** (W-4.5 miles)

At A Glance

FEATURED BRANDS	Chicken Cock, High West, Jefferson's *(all produced for other vendors)*
OWNER	Bardstown Bourbon Co.
REGION	Bardstown
AVAILABLE TO TOUR	Fermenters, Column Stills, Warehouse
COST	$$$ - Military and Senior Discounts
LOCATION	1500 Parkway Dr, Bardstown, KY 40004
WEBSITE	*www.bardstownbourbon.com*

Drew's Top Three Reasons to Visit

1 While in the warehouse, they gave us the opportunity to remove the plug (known as a bung stopper) from a barrel of rye whiskey. A whiskey thief was used to extract the maturing spirit and we were all given a sample.

2 If you have trouble multitasking, imagine having over 40 different recipes to keep straight. The computerized system is something to behold.

3 Their bar and restaurant are well worth a visit, even if you don't have time for a tour. The food is excellent and the bar features selections from around the globe.

MORE INFORMATION: *www.whiskey-lore.com/bardstownbourbonco*

Barton 1792 Distillery

ABOUT BARTON 1792

Drive into Bardstown and it is hard to miss the Barton 1792 semitrucks wheeling through town. Their side panels beckon you to take a complimentary tour of the distillery. This is no gimmick. It is a full-fledged free distillery experience, which enables you to see the industrial side of production. The experience finishes with a free guided tasting.

The standard tour lasts about an hour and your guide will start with a detailed history of the distillery. From there, you enter a warehouse, see the milling process, and crane your neck to see the massive column still. At one point, you will climb several flights of stairs to see the results of distillation—there I had a chance to sample white dog.

For those that want to go even deeper, reserve your spot on the extensive Estate Tour. This tour is also free and is the deepest dive I have taken at any distillery. It is also the only way to have your picture taken with the world's largest bourbon barrel. The tour runs once per day and they limit participants, so reserve in advance.

LISTEN/WATCH FOR

Look for the limestone siding in the area connected to the brick distillery. This is the boiler room and it is the last remaining feature from the original 1879 structure.

2020 TASTING EXPERIENCE/KEEPSAKES*

We started off with the guided tasting of 80 proof Very Old Barton. We also tasted the flagship 1792 Kentucky Straight Bourbon along with a sample bourbon ball from Muth's of Louisville. The tasting finished with Barton's Chocolate Bourbon Ball Cream Liqueur. At the end of the tour they gave us a bunghole plug keepsake, stamped with the date of the tour.

GETTING THERE

There are two different entrances into the distillery. One is off of US 31E for people coming from the south and the other is off of US 62 with signage pointing down Barton Road. There is a sign that says to stop if you are a truck or vendor. It does not mean tourists have to stop—you can proceed.

TOUR SCHEDULE

9 a.m.–3 p.m. Mon–Sat
Various tours are available. No set time.

SIDE TRIPS

- **Old Talbott Tavern** - Step inside the world's oldest bourbon bar and end your day with a flight of whiskeys from around the area.
- **Oscar Getz Whiskey Museum** - Enjoy former Barton's owner Oscar Getz's amazing collection of old whiskey bottles and other whiskey memorabilia.

CLOSEST DISTILLERIES

- **Heaven Hill Bourbon Heritage Center** (SE-1.6 miles)
- **Preservation Distillery** (S-1.6 miles)

At A Glance

FEATURED BRANDS	1792, Kentucky Gentleman, Kentucky Tavern, Very Old Barton
OWNER	Sazerac
REGION	Bardstown
AVAILABLE TO TOUR	Fermenters, Column Stills, Warehouse
COST	Free
LOCATION	300 Barton Rd, Bardstown, KY 40004
WEBSITE	*www.1792distillery.com*

Drew's Top Three Reasons to Visit

1 Along with Buffalo Trace, this is the best value in Kentucky: a great, free tour with complimentary tastings, and enhanced experiences that are also free.

2 Bourbon history fans will enjoy this tour. The roots of the current distillery date back to 1879 when it was the Tom Moore Distillery. The tour highlights the evolution of the distillery and the brand.

3 There are plenty of fancy new tourist-friendly distilleries, but this one gets you into the real and gritty side of bourbon production.

MORE INFORMATION: *www.whiskey-lore.com/barton1792*

Boone County Distillery

ABOUT BOONE COUNTY DISTILLERY

The original Boone County Distillery opened in 1833 near the banks of the Ohio River. After being shut down in 1910, the brand remained a distant memory until the current owners re-established the distillery in 2015. They honor the craft and inspiration of their forefathers with the slogan "Made by Ghosts®."

Sitting in an office park, two miles off the main highway, Boone County Distillery will give you a bit of a Clark Kent to Superman moment when you first walk in the door. The outside industrial park feel gives way to a warm and stylish visitor's center. Look beyond the glass and you will see a full-featured production facility distilling bourbon, rye, and gin.

Your tour will take you from the hammer mill through the production process, and finishes in the warehouse just behind the main building. They reward you at the end with a guided tasting that goes beyond bourbon.

LISTEN/WATCH FOR

Look out for "The Bear." It is a hybrid still that gets its name from a real bear. Ask and they will tell you about the bear and the man who inspired the story.

2020 TASTING EXPERIENCE/KEEPSAKES*

The tasting event started with white dog. But rather than taste it they asked me to rub it in my hands. This showed how the aroma evolves as you add friction. We tried the 100% rye Tanner's Curse at 120 proof, the bourbon version of Tanner's Curse, the eight-year-old bourbon, and finished with the Bourbon Cream. They provided pretzels to help cleanse the palate between tastes, and I received a branded shot glass as a keepsake.

GETTING THERE

If you are driving between Cincinnati and Lexington, KY on I-75 then you will see the sign for Boone County Distillery. It is a little bit off the road with a few twists and turns, so have your GPS handy. There is plenty of paved parking around the distillery.

TOUR SCHEDULE

10:30 a.m.–4:15 p.m. Tue–Sat;
Noon–4:15 p.m. Sun
Various tours are available.

SIDE TRIPS

- **Ark Encounter** - Imagine seeing a recreation of Noah's Ark in Northern Kentucky. This is it, along with a zoo and various events. At the time of writing, kids aged ten and under are free.
- **Verona Vineyards and Estate Bistro**
  A farm vineyard located just south of the I-75/I-71 split in Verona, KY.

CLOSEST DISTILLERIES

- **Second Sight Spirits** (N-17.1 miles)
- **New Riff Distilling** (N-18.6 miles)

At A Glance

FEATURED BRANDS	Boone County
OWNER	Boone County Distilling Co.
REGION	North
AVAILABLE TO TOUR	Milling, Fermenters, Hybrid Still, Bottling, Warehouse
COST	$
LOCATION	10601 Toebben Dr, Independence, KY 410511
WEBSITE	*www.boonedistilling.com*

Drew's Top Three Reasons to Visit

1 Boone County has done an excellent job researching the history of the old distillery, crafting some entertaining stories of bears and burial grounds– but no ghosts.

2 I found the staff very personable, knowledgeable, and willing to answer any questions about their process and history.

3 You get an excellent review of the milling process, something many distilleries neglect. They are also one of the few distilleries I have seen with a hybrid still.

MORE INFORMATION: *www.whiskey-lore.com/boonecounty*

Buffalo Trace Distillery

ABOUT BUFFALO TRACE DISTILLERY

Buffalo Trace whiskey is so awarded and so popular that most of their brands are now sold on allocation. This means you usually have to ask your local retailer to either hold you a bottle or let you know the next time it is coming in. The distillery is in the middle of a major expansion that should help ease some supply versus demand issues in the distant future. For now, Buffalo Trace brands remain high on collector's lists.

The distillery has a long and storied history going back to 1775 when Hancock and Willis Lee began a distilling operation. You will see banners proudly proclaiming their listing on the National Register of Historic Places; it also holds the designation as a National Historic Landmark. Many of the brands feature the names of former owners and distillers like Albert Blanton, Colonel E. H. Taylor, and George T. Stagg.

This complementary tour features a film history, a walk through the campus, and an extensive focus on warehousing before concluding with a guided tasting above the gift shop. I will warn you though, allocated bourbons are not for sale at the distillery.

LISTEN/WATCH FOR

Listen to how the construction of the warehouse and placing the barrels in that warehouse can have a heavy influence on the quality and speed of maturation.

2020 TASTING EXPERIENCE/KEEPSAKES*

For a free tour, the samples are quite liberal. They guided us through a tasting of Wheatley Vodka, White Dog from Mash Bill #1, Buffalo Trace, and Eagle Rare, finishing with their Bourbon Cream. There are no keepsakes but bear in mind that this is a free tour.

GETTING THERE

Buffalo Trace is directly north of Kentucky's capital city of Frankfort. If you are coming from Lexington, you can loop around to it by taking Exit 58 off I-64. From Louisville, Exit 53B will be your best bet. There is plenty of parking, but make sure you follow the signs to the visitor's parking area, as it is very easy to end up in employee parking.

TOUR SCHEDULE

9 a.m.–4 p.m. Mon–Sat; Noon–3 p.m. Sun
Various tours are available.
Hourly or when needed.

SIDE TRIPS

- **Kentucky Gentlemen Cigar Company** Cigar aficionados will find a fine selection, including the unique experience of bourbon enhanced cigars.
- **Kentucky State Capitol** - Built in 1910, the state capitol buil ing is open for guided tours.

CLOSEST DISTILLERIES

- **Glenns Creek Distilling** (S-6.8 miles)
- **Castle & Key Distillery** (S-7.6 miles)

At A Glance

FEATURED BRANDS	Ancient Age, Benchmark, Blanton's, Buffalo Trace, Eagle Rare, E.H. Taylor, George T. Stagg, Hancock's President Reserve, Old Charter, Old Rip Van Winkle, Pappy Van Winkle, Rock Hill Farms, Sazerac Rye
OWNER	Sazerac
REGION	Central
AVAILABLE TO TOUR	Warehouse, Bottling
COST	Free
LOCATION	113 Great Buffalo Trace, Frankfort, KY 40601
WEBSITE	*www.buffalotracedistillery.com*

Drew's Top Three Reasons to Visit

1   You don't need a reservation for the standard tour, and tours go when needed. (If you want to go on a specialty tour like their free ghost tour or the warehouse tours, you will need to book months in advance.)

2   You will see the Blanton's bottling room, where each bottle is hand-filled, labeled, and boxed. They even let you ask the employees questions. Just make sure you don't get in the way of production.

3   The campus is full of history and great for Instagram shots. Get a photo with the water tower, or go see the big white bison near the Elmer T. Lee Clubhouse.

MORE INFORMATION: *www.whiskey-lore.com/buffalotrace*

Bulleit Distilling Company

ABOUT BULLEIT DISTILLING COMPANY

One of the newest mass-production distilleries in Kentucky, Bulleit is going all-in on distilling in the countryside. Located just north of I-64 between Louisville and Lexington, you navigate some scenic country roads on your way to this state-of-the-art whiskey campus. Bulleit gives you an opportunity to step away from the historic and craft tours available elsewhere to see a distillery built for large-scale production.

The tour begins in the elegant, yet rustic visitor's center, where you are told the history of Bulleit and about its leadership. You are then taken by bus to the production facility, where you get the opportunity to walk into a room filled with fermenters, as well as the milling room. One of your first stops will be the control room, where a team manages and monitors the distilling process from this central location.

After the tour, you will enjoy a unique multi-sensory tasting experience. The tour empties into the beautiful gift shop with plenty of bourbon and rye for sale. There is also a cocktail bar where they offer cocktail crafting classes on select Wednesdays and Sundays.

LISTEN/WATCH FOR

Look for the wall featuring the Yeast Library: here you can see the five strains of yeast that Bulleit uses and the characteristics they provide to the spirits. This is one of only a couple distilleries in Kentucky using this many yeast strains.

2020 TASTING EXPERIENCE/KEEPSAKES*

They gave us four different samples of whiskey: the Bulleit Kentucky Straight Bourbon, 95 Rye, 10 Year Bourbon, and Barrel Strength. Next to each whiskey there was what looked like a pepper shaker: each shaker contained a scent found in the matched bourbon or rye.

GETTING THERE

This is one of those locations that will require GPS. It is far from the main highway but the roads to it are in good condition. However, because the distillery was so new when I visited, they didn't have extensive signage. I would imagine this is now resolved.

TOUR SCHEDULE

9:30 a.m.–4 p.m. Tue–Thu & Sun;
9:30 a.m.–5 p.m. Fri & Sat
Various tours are available.
No specific schedule.

SIDE TRIPS

- **FRP LaGrange Quarry** - A local rock quarry that has been repurposed into a summer water recreation area including swimming and scuba diving.
- **Smith-Berry Vineyard & Winery** Award-winning winery with tastings offered.

CLOSEST DISTILLERIES

- **Jeptha Creed Distillery** (W-9.8 miles)
- **Three Boys Distillery** (SE-12.5 miles)

At A Glance

FEATURED BRANDS	Bulleit
OWNER	Diageo
REGION	Central
AVAILABLE TO TOUR	Milling, Fermenters, Column Still
COST	$$$ - Military and minors free
LOCATION	3464 Benson Pike, Shelbyville, KY 40065
WEBSITE	*www.bulleit.com*

Drew's Top Three Reasons to Visit

1 The sensory tasting experience is great for those just getting into the nosing and tasting of whiskey. Here you get to smell what you're going to smell before you smell it.

2 Column stills are the heart of a large-scale distillation process. This is one of the few tours that shows you inside a column still, which gives you a visual representation of how they work.

3 This place is a feast for the eyeballs from the moment you walk in the door. Sit and relax in their well-appointed greeting area or grab a cocktail before your tour begins.

MORE INFORMATION: *www.whiskey-lore.com/bulleit*

Casey Jones Distillery

ABOUT CASEY JONES DISTILLERY

Take a trip back 100 years, to a time when Casey Jones mastered his still-making craft at Golden Pond. In a country that was "dry" during Prohibition, he was the moonshiner's go-to man when they needed easy to transport stills. Casey's grandson A. J. and his wife Peg have brought this legacy to the Casey Jones Distillery.

Located just north of Hopkinsville in rural Kentucky, they are creating modern moonshines and bourbons using the same coffin-still design his grandfather perfected in the days of the bootleggers.

For a real treat, see the coffin pot still the Federal Government commissioned Casey to make for their Land Between the Lakes National Recreation Area—it rests above the bar in the Distillery Lounge. During the tour, learn about Casey's two stints at the Mill Point Federal Penitentiary, and then enjoy a tasting of their Small Batch Bourbon and a wide selection of moonshines. If it is a nice day, take a stroll down by the lake after your tour.

LISTEN/WATCH FOR

While you are on the tour, look for the photo of Mill Point Federal Penitentiary and listen for the unique nickname it earned because of who stayed there.

2020 TASTING EXPERIENCE/KEEPSAKES*

After a look around the distillery, they offered me a choice of several moonshines and bourbons. They also had bourbon- and rye-finished moonshines. Many of these spirits have interesting names like Total Eclipse, which commemorates the eponymous 2017 event that passed over the distillery. I also received a branded shot glass as a keepsake and collected my Stateline Whiskey Tour stave (more details in my top three reasons).

GETTING THERE

You will most likely want to depend on your GPS. Casey Jones Distilling has plenty of road signs pointing to it, but with its rural setting it's always good to have GPS as a backup. There is a long well-kept gravel drive leading to the distillery, with plenty of parking.

TOUR SCHEDULE

10 a.m.–5 p.m. Mon–Sat; Noon–5 p.m. Sun
Various tours are available.
Hourly, on the hour.

SIDE TRIPS

- **Land Between the Lakes National Recreation Area** - A wonderful place for hiking, mountain biking, camping, and seeing amazing wildlife. If you have never seen elk or bison, this is the place to go.
- **Hopkinsville Brewing Company** - Head to downtown Hopkinsville to unwind with a craft brew, local food provided by food trucks, and local entertainment.
- **Christian Way Farm & Mini Golf** A family-friendly petting zoo and mini-golf center. Seasonal business.

CLOSEST DISTILLERIES

- **MB Roland Distillery** (SE-22.2 miles)
- **Crooked Tail Distilling** (NW-25.6 miles)

At A Glance

FEATURED BRANDS	Casey Jones Small Batch Bourbon
OWNER	Stillworks LLC
REGION	West
AVAILABLE TO TOUR	Coffin Pot Still, Warehouse, Bottling
COST	$
LOCATION	2815 Witty Ln, Hopkinsville, KY 42240
WEBSITE	*www.caseyjonesdistillery.com*

Drew's Top Three Reasons to Visit

1 Western Kentucky distilleries take a little more effort to get to, but three distilleries (Casey Jones, MB Roland, and Old Glory) have banded together to offer you a nice gift for going out of your way. On the Stateline Whiskey Tour, each distillery will provide you with a stamp and a shot glass. When you get all three stamps, you receive a nice wood stave to hold your glasses.

2 This is a chance to see a unique piece of moonshining history. I haven't seen square coffin pot stills at any other distillery I have visited.

3 A true craft distillery. It is highly likely that you will interact with the owners.

MORE INFORMATION: *www.whiskey-lore.com/caseyjones*

Castle & Key Distillery

ABOUT CASTLE & KEY DISTILLERY

Is that a castle sitting in the middle of bourbon country? Yes, it is. After moving on from the Old Fire Copper Distillery (now Buffalo Trace) in 1887, Colonel E. H. Taylor Jr. had this distillery built as a showplace. Abandoned in 1972, the distillery sat idle for years and was being dismantled for scrap. It took the vision and investment of Will Arvin and Wes Murry to preserve the distillery and bring this magnificent property back to life.

At the time of writing in 2020, Castle & Key tours were focusing on gin as their bourbon had not yet reached maturity. I have attempted to keep this guide to just distilleries where you can try bourbons, but no tour of Kentucky would be complete without seeing the vision of Col. E.H. Taylor Jr.—a bourbon legend.

I took the higher-priced tour because it includes a walk through the sunken garden and down to Warehouse B, the world's longest rickhouse. The smaller tour focuses entirely on the distillery. Both tours end with a cocktail and a walk through the gift shop.

LISTEN/WATCH FOR

Be on the lookout for Rick Key, the white and beige rescue cat that patrols the distillery property. Also, while in the gift shop, see if you can spot the photo showing the property in 1903.

2020 TASTING EXPERIENCE/KEEPSAKES*

They took us to the bar area and talked about the different botanicals and syrups used to make their gin and vodka cocktails. After a sample of the gin, we chose from a menu of unique creations. The tour ticket you receive feels like a golden ticket from a Wonka Bar. There were no other keepsakes.

GETTING THERE

Located south of Frankfort, down narrow McCracken Pike, you will find Castle & Key nestled between Woodford Reserve and Glenns Creek Distillery. You can't miss it. The castle is right up against the highway with parking available across the street.

TOUR SCHEDULE

10 a.m.–4 p.m. Wed–Sat; 11 a.m.–4 p.m. Sun Various tours are available. No set time. Hourly, on the hour. Check for seasonal changes.

SIDE TRIPS

- **Daniel Boone's Grave** - Part of Frankfort Cemetery, this is one of Daniel Boone's two grave sites (the other is in Missouri). In 1845, Daniel and his wife Rebecca's remains were moved from the grave site in Marthasville, MO but there is some dispute as to whether they moved the right remains.
- **Kentucky History Center & Museums** Head to downtown Frankfort and use the History Center as a jumping-off point for immersing yourself in the state's history.

CLOSEST DISTILLERIES

- **Glenns Creek Distilling** (W-0.8 miles)
- **Woodford Reserve** (S-3.3 miles)

At A Glance

FEATURED BRANDS	Not available (bourbon still aging)
OWNER	Peristyle LLC
REGION	Central
AVAILABLE TO TOUR	Milling, Fermenters, Column Still
COST	$$$ - Military discount
LOCATION	4445 McCracken Pike, Frankfort, KY 40601
WEBSITE	*www.castleandkey.com*

Drew's Top Three Reasons to Visit

1 Interior portions of the old distillery are being refurbished, including the fermenters used by its post-Prohibition owners National Distillers, allowing a glimpse of yesteryear.

2 John Carloftis, famous for his rooftop gardens in New York City, designed the distillery's beautiful Sunken Garden.

3 Colonel Taylor's vision was to recreate a Scottish castle, and he did an excellent job.

MORE INFORMATION: *www.whiskey-lore.com/castleandkey*

Four Roses Distillery

ABOUT FOUR ROSES DISTILLERY

Built in 1910 and listed on the National Register of Historic Places, Four Roses Distillery is a unique experience in bourbon country. Its Spanish Mission architecture harkens back to a style that was all the rage in Southern California in the early 20th century. Recent renovations are complete and the renovated distillery is a highlight of the tour.

Four Roses has a fascinating history. What started as a whiskey rectifying business evolved into the most popular bourbon of post World War II America. But in the mid-1950s it inexplicably disappeared from American shelves, until master distiller Jim Rutledge and the Japanese firm Kirin brought it back to the United States in 2002.

During a short film, you will hear the legend that brought Four Roses its name, before heading to the historic distillery to learn about their bourbon-making process. At the end of the tour there is a guided tasting and a description of their ten recipes.

LISTEN/WATCH FOR

Four Roses' former owner Seagram's purchased several distilleries in Kentucky. The heritage yeast strains from each of these distilleries is featured in Four Roses' bourbons. Listen for how they combine these yeast strains with their two mash bills to create their different styles of bourbon.

2020 TASTING EXPERIENCE/KEEPSAKES*

At the end of the tour we sampled Four Roses (sometimes referred to as Yellow Label), Four Roses Single Barrel, and Four Roses Small Batch. They also gave us a nice sturdy drinking glass, perfect for enjoying a bourbon on the rocks.

GETTING THERE

If you are heading down from Frankfort, the distillery is just past Lawrenceburg on US 127. If you come from Lexington, head out on US 60 to the Bluegrass Parkway. It's not too difficult to find and there is ample parking at the visitor's center. Lawrenceburg is also an excellent jumping-off point for Wild Turkey and Woodford Reserve. Just head down Bonds Mill Road and look for the signs.

TOUR SCHEDULE

9:30 a.m.–3:30 p.m. Mon–Sat;
11:30 a.m.–3:30 p.m. Sun
Hourly, on the hour. Closed June-August, hours may be modified. Call ahead.

SIDE TRIPS

- **Four Roses Warehouse** - Make sure to hold onto your ticket for free entry into the warehouse facility.
- **Martha Layne Collins Bluegrass Parkway** - A beautiful drive through Kentucky on a highway that was once a toll road, but ceased charging when it's bond was paid off in 1991.

CLOSEST DISTILLERIES

- **Wild Turkey** (NE-8.1 miles)
- **Woodford Reserve** (N-18.8 miles)

At A Glance

FEATURED BRANDS	Four Roses
OWNER	Kirin
REGION	Central
AVAILABLE TO TOUR	Fermenters, Column Still
COST	$$ - Military and minors free
LOCATION	1224 Bonds Mill Rd, Lawrenceburg, KY 40342
WEBSITE	*www.fourrosesbourbon.com*

Drew's Top Three Reasons to Visit

1 The Spanish Mission architecture runs throughout the distillery campus. Take some extra time to stroll around and take pictures. Just watch out for cars and trucks.

2 The gift shop contains some historic pieces from Four Roses' glory days and Prohibition, so take a little extra time to look around.

3 Your ticket purchase here also gets you free access and an additional tasting at the Four Roses Warehouse in Cox Creek (50 miles west).

MORE INFORMATION: *www.whiskey-lore.com/fourroses*

Glenns Creek Distillery

ABOUT GLENNS CREEK DISTILLERY

If you want formula tours and state-of-the-art distilling, look elsewhere. If you want to find passionate distillers, who are serious about making craft whiskey and showing you that process, then check out Glenns Creek Distillery. This is what it is like in the craft-distilling trenches, and you will see each step of the process. If you are lucky, you might be invited to join in a step or two.

During my visit, I mentioned my love for whiskey history, and they amazed me with their wealth of knowledge. They also provide a lot of background on the Old Crow Distillery that sits directly behind Glenns Creek Distillery.

One of their most interesting spirits is OCD #5. Those initials should look familiar as they come from the Old Crow Distillery, as does the wild yeast strain they use in this bourbon. They took the yeast from fermentation tank #5 in the abandoned distillery. Is it the original strain? That is hard to say, but it's a cool story.

LISTEN/WATCH FOR

Check out the bottle of white dog they sell with Alexander Hamilton's picture on it. There is a story that comes along with it. Ask them what they think about ol' Alex and his tax policies.

2020 TASTING EXPERIENCE/KEEPSAKES*

I tried four of their products: the double-oaked, single-barrel bourbon Stave + Barrel, OCD #5, Prohibition Kentucky Rum, and Ryesky Rye. They have since added a new bourbon, a vodka, and a grain and sugar cane spirit. There were no keepsakes from the tour, but you can use your admission as credit towards a bottle of their spirits.

GETTING THERE

If you have ever been to Scotland, a drive down McCracken Pike from Frankfort will transport you back there: the route is similar to the single track roads found in the Highlands—there are blind curves and the road is very narrow (by American standards). The distillery is close to Castle & Key and Woodford Reserve; combining the three could make for a nice afternoon of touring. An excellent way to finish is with dinner at a local creekside restaurant called The Stave.

TOUR SCHEDULE

10 a.m.–4 p.m. Mon–Sat; 1–4 p.m. Sun
Hourly, on the hour.

SIDE TRIPS

- **Clyde E. Buckley Wildlife Sanctuary & Life Adventure Center** - Walk the trails and enjoy the sounds of nature.
- **Kentucky Vietnam Veteran's Memorial** Honoring the troops who gave their lives. Also an excellent spot to view the State Capitol from a distance. Watch for deer.

CLOSEST DISTILLERIES

- **Castle & Key Distillery** (E-0.8 miles)
- **Woodford Reserve** (SE-4.2 miles)

At A Glance

FEATURED BRANDS	OCD #5, Ryskey, Stave+Barrel
OWNER	Glenns Creek Distilling
REGION	Central
AVAILABLE TO TOUR	Fermenters, Pot Still, Warehouse
COST	$
LOCATION	3501 McCracken Pike, Frankfort, KY 40601
WEBSITE	*www.glennscreekdistillery.com*

Drew's Top Three Reasons to Visit

1 If you are a rebel at heart, you will enjoy the independent attitude present at this distillery. I was told I shouldn't be surprised if I saw a Jolly Roger flag flying above the distillery.

2 This isn't a large facility, and you can just about see it all from where you sit to do the tasting.

3 There is something about the stripped-down nature of this experience that had me recommending it to others. It flies a bit under the radar.

MORE INFORMATION: *www.whiskey-lore.com/glennscreek*

Heaven Hill Bourbon Heritage Center

ABOUT HEAVEN HILL BOURBON HERITAGE CENTER

The large distillery whose name escapes most casual bourbon drinkers is Heaven Hill. But say names like Elijah Craig and Evan Williams and suddenly you grab their attention. Heaven Hill is the sixth largest producer of spirits in the United States, and the largest family-owned distillery based in Kentucky.

At the time of writing, the Heaven Hill Bourbon Heritage Center was undergoing a major renovation. However, though they have packed away the artifacts that were previously on display, there is still plenty to enjoy about this facility. The standard tour takes you to the warehouse and gives you an overview of the distillery's history.

The tasting includes a nice cross-section of their product line. I recommend spending a couple more bucks to do the Whiskey Connoisseur's guided tasting. This does not include a tour of the rickhouse; instead, you will taste four top-shelf spirits from the Heaven Hill family.

LISTEN/WATCH FOR

Look out for plumb bobs in the rickhouse: these hang down from the roof and point to a circle near the floor. These detect any leaning issues with the warehouse.

2020 TASTING EXPERIENCE/KEEPSAKES*

We started the standard tour tasting with their wheated bourbon, Larceny, followed by the very popular Elijah Craig Small Batch, and finishing with Rittenhouse Bottled-in-Bond Rye. They also gave us a tasty bourbon ball to enjoy. I received no keepsakes from this tour; I did, however, receive a tasting glass from the Whiskey Connoisseur's experience.

GETTING THERE

Located just south of Bardstown and near Willett Distillery, it's worth using your GPS to reach the distillery. There is a large parking lot. Construction is expected until early 2021, so things may change.

TOUR SCHEDULE

10:15 a.m.–3:15 p.m. Tue–Sat;
12:15 p.m.–2:15 p.m. Sun
Various tours are available.

SIDE TRIPS

- **Abbey of Gethsemani** - Visit the beautiful site where French Trappist monks first settled in the area. The buildings date back to the 1850s and it is still an active monastery that holds services and has a gift shop.
- **Lincoln Homestead State Park** - You can see the original home of Abraham Lincoln's mother Nancy Hanks and a reconstruction of both the Lincoln Cabin and his father's workshop. Free

CLOSEST DISTILLERIES

- **Willett Distillery** (SE-1.3 miles)
- **Barton 1792** (W-1.6 miles)

At A Glance

FEATURED BRANDS	Bernheim, Cabin Still, Elijah Craig, Evan Williams, Fighting Cock, J.T.S. Brown, Heaven Hill, Henry McKenna, Mellow Corn, Old Fitzgerald, Pikesville, Rittenhouse Rye
OWNER	Heaven Hill
REGION	Bardstown
AVAILABLE TO TOUR	Warehouse
COST	$$ - Minors free
LOCATION	1311 Gilkey Run Rd, Bardstown, KY 40004
WEBSITE	*www.heavenhilldistillery.com*

Drew's Top Three Reasons to Visit

1 If you like Kentucky spirits, then you most likely already enjoy one of Heaven Hill's products. In addition to Evan Williams, other brands they produce include Larceny, Rittenhouse Rye, Pikesville, etc.

2 A walk in that historic warehouse is a treat, and the guide does a nice job of explaining how whiskey ages.

3 With a number of historic brands like Henry McKenna, J.W. Dant, and Old Fitzgerald, there is a lot of potential to educate visitors about the whiskey and pioneers of Nelson County and Kentucky.

MORE INFORMATION: *www.whiskey-lore.com/heavenhill*

James E. Pepper Distillery

ABOUT JAMES E. PEPPER DISTILLERY

In 2008, Amir Peay saw an opportunity to take an abandoned distillery and restore its history, develop a craft distillery, and make it a showplace surrounded by music, food, and entertainment. Today, James E. Pepper Distillery is the centerpiece of north Lexington's Distillery District.

While James E. Pepper celebrates its past through its 1776 branded bourbon and rye, they also embrace their standing as a craft distillery with some highly inventive mash bills.

The tour begins with a walk through the distillery museum. Your guide introduces you to the stories of Kentucky Colonel James E. Pepper, his wife Ella, and the historic origins of the property. As the tour continues, you walk through a day in the life of a distillery, as they unveil the whiskey making process from start to finish. At one point you are encouraged to sample both their new-make spirit and their aged product, pulled straight from the barrel.

LISTEN/WATCH FOR

It is suggested that a bartender at the Pendennis Club in Louisville crafted the "Old Fashioned Cocktail" in honor of Colonel James E. Pepper. Colonel Pepper returned the favor by introducing the cocktail to the Waldorf-Astoria in New York City. You can enjoy the original drink on-site for an extra charge.

2020 TASTING EXPERIENCE/KEEPSAKES*

After tasting the rye straight from the barrel, we sampled their 1776 Rye Whiskey (100 Proof) in the tasting room. We also received chocolate that contained rye whiskey-soaked walnuts. In addition, we tasted their 1776 Bourbon, which is a high rye (36% rye content). They gave us a branded Glencairn tasting glass as a keepsake.

GETTING THERE

You will find the distillery just north of downtown Lexington. The area is branded as the Distillery District: while it may feel like an industrial area, this is becoming a hot spot for food, drinks, and entertainment. Parking is not an issue; there is a large parking lot behind the distillery and a smaller unmarked parking area across the street.

TOUR SCHEDULE

10:30 a.m.–3:30 p.m. Wed–Sat;
Noon–4 p.m. Sun
Various tours are available. Hourly.
Winter hours differ.

SIDE TRIPS

- **Fusion Brewing** - Tour the brewery or hang out and enjoy some of their creative brews.
- **Keeneland Race Course** - What would a trip to Kentucky be without horses and horse racing? Here is where great thoroughbreds get their start.

CLOSEST DISTILLERIES

- **Barrel House Distilling** (SE-0.1 miles)
- **Town Branch Distillery** (W-2.3 miles)

At A Glance

FEATURED BRANDS	1776, Old Pepper, Henry Clay Whiskey
OWNER	James E. Pepper
REGION	Lexington
AVAILABLE TO TOUR	Milling, Fermenters, Column Still, Bottling
COST	$$$ - Military and minors free
LOCATION	1228 Manchester St #100, Lexington, KY 40504
WEBSITE	*www.jamesepepper.com*

Drew's Top Three Reasons to Visit

1 The guides here are well versed on the stories of Colonel Pepper and his wife, and the distillery comes alive visually and through an excellent oral history.

2 We sampled a unique mash bill that contained 51% corn and 49% malted barley. I also saw an experimental peated single malt barrel. The creative nature of the distillery makes it worth investigating.

3 Start your day in the Distillery District with a tour, then enjoy lunch or dinner at Goodfellas Pizzeria. Enjoy an ice cream at Crank & Boom, then head to The Burl for an evening of music and entertainment.

MORE INFORMATION: *www.whiskey-lore.com/jamesepepper*

Jeptha Creed Distillery

ABOUT JEPTHA CREED DISTILLERY

Jeptha Creed is a stylish farm-based "ground-to-glass" distillery and event center located just off I-64, between Louisville and Lexington. This family-owned distillery has at its core the mother-daughter team of Joyce and Autumn Nethery. Joyce is the Master Distiller, while co-owner Autumn handles marketing and is the youngest distillery owner in Kentucky.

What makes Jeptha Creed different is a unique locally grown, non-GMO grain called Bloody Butcher corn. This heirloom variety of corn caught the family's attention when they noticed it was becoming the favorite snack of local wildlife. This is at the heart of the mash bill that is used into their bourbon, moonshine, and vodka.

The distillery tour features a view of the porch and outdoor event space before passing the distillery cats' home. There is a short video talking about the distillery and the family, then they take you through production and finish up your journey with a tasting. The tour takes around 30 minutes.

LISTEN/WATCH FOR

During the tour, keep an ear out for the origin story of the name Jeptha Creed. There are ties back to Scotland and Kentucky's favorite son Daniel Boone.

2020 TASTING EXPERIENCE/KEEPSAKES*

During the tasting experience I was given the opportunity to pick out several spirits to try. There was a variety of Kentucky moonshines, vodkas, and their Kentucky Straight 4-Grain Bourbon. Released in 2019, the bourbon includes Bloody Butcher corn, rye, wheat, and malted barley in the mash bill. Since my visit they have added Pawpaw Brandy. I received a Jeptha Creed shot glass as a keepsake.

GETTING THERE

The distillery is just off of I-64 between Louisville and Lexington. Take Exit 32 and follow the signs. There is plenty of parking.

TOUR SCHEDULE

11 a.m.–5 p.m. Tue–Sat; Noon–4 p.m. Sun Tours on the hours (on the half hour on Saturdays). Winter hours may vary.

SIDE TRIPS

- **Abraham Lincoln's Boyhood Home at Knob Creek (National Park Service)** See where the 16th President of the United States was born. In the summer rangers provide guided tours. Free.
- **Louisville Mega Cavern -** Your underground adventure spot in Louisville with zip lining, electric bike tours, and a tram tour. Located near the airport.

CLOSEST DISTILLERIES

- **Bulleit Distilling Co.** (E-9.1 miles)
- **Three Boys Distillery** (E-18.6 miles)

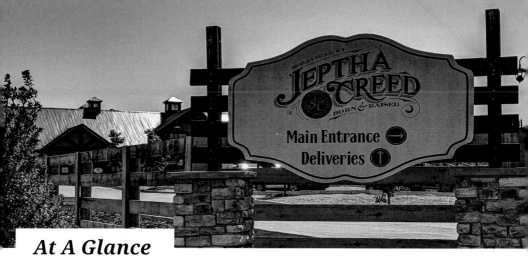

At A Glance

FEATURED BRANDS	Jeptha Creed
OWNER	Rut 'N Strut Distillery
REGION	Central
AVAILABLE TO TOUR	Fermenters, Column Still, Hybrid Still Bottling
COST	$$ - Children free and minors discount
LOCATION	500 Gordon Lane, Shelbyville, KY 40065
WEBSITE	*www.jepthacreed.com*

Drew's Top Three Reasons to Visit

1 If you're looking for something to do in central Kentucky, check their calendar for events, including Jammin' at Jeptha on Friday nights.

2 They have a nice restaurant and cocktail bar on-site. Stop in for a bite to eat, even if you don't have time for a tour.

3 Check out all the classic vehicles. There is a 1915 Ford Model T and a 1932 Ford Truck. There is even a classic truck in the gift shop.

MORE INFORMATION: *www.whiskey-lore.com/jepthacreed*

Jim Beam American Stillhouse

ABOUT JIM BEAM AMERICAN STILLHOUSE

If you are expecting a large corporate tour that keeps you at arm's length, you are in for a surprise at the Jim Beam American Stillhouse. Yes, Jim Beam is a global brand producing hundreds of thousands of barrels of whiskey each year, but the scenic campus and diverse tour will make you feel right at home.

When you reach the visitor's center, have your photo taken with the bronze statue of Jim Beam. Walk inside, get your ticket, and absorb the history of America's first family of bourbon. After a short bus ride, you will arrive at a small craft distillery. This smaller-scale setup is more conducive to showing the bourbon making process. Finish with a chance to bottle your own Knob Creek and enjoy a guided tasting. This is one of the longer standard tours in Kentucky, lasting around 90 minutes.

To make the day complete, enjoy a tasting at the Jim Beam Bourbon Bar or head to Fred's Smokehouse for some barbecue. And don't forget to get your photo taken with a bronze likeness of Booker Noe in a rocking chair, along with his dog Dot.

LISTEN/WATCH FOR

See if you can spot Jim Beam's old yeast jug from 1935. It is a copper vessel that sits in a corner, on the first floor of the craft distillery. They still use it today.

2020 TASTING EXPERIENCE/KEEPSAKES*

There was a well-represented cross-section of Jim Beam products in the tasting room. They gave us three samples: Jim Beam Double Aged Black and Knob Creek 100 Proof Small Batch Bourbon to start, and then a choice from the other displayed spirits for our last sample. I went for the Bookers. They also gave us a little branded American Stillhouse tasting glass as a keepsake.

GETTING THERE

The American Stillhouse is very easy to find, just off of Exit 112 on I-65. Head east and you will see the white Jim Beam barn on the left-hand side of the road. If you are coming up from Bardstown, you will first see the business entrance first—just head on to the next entrance.

TOUR SCHEDULE

9:30 a.m.–3:30 p.m. Mon–Sat;
12:30 p.m.–3:00 p.m. Sun
Times vary. Make sure you get your online reservations at least 48 hours in advance. Walk ups are possible but tours do sell out.

SIDE TRIPS

- **Bernheim Arboretum and Research** Stop by for a snack or lunch at Issac's Cafe, learn about the Bernheim Forest or go for a nice walk or bike ride on the 40 miles of trails.
- **Forest Edge Winery** - For a change of pace, head here for a local wine tasting.

CLOSEST DISTILLERIES

- **Barton 1792 Distillery** (SE-15.4 miles)
- **Heaven Hill Bourbon Heritage Center** (SE-17.0 miles)

At A Glance

FEATURED BRANDS	Bakers, Basil Hayden, Bookers, Jim Beam, Knob Creek, Legent, Old Crow, Old Grand-dad, Old Overholt
OWNER	Beam Suntory
REGION	Bardstown
AVAILABLE TO TOUR	Fermenters, Column Still, Bottling
COST	$$ Children free and minors discount
LOCATION	568 Happy Hollow Road, Clermont, KY 40110
WEBSITE	*www.jimbeam.com*

Drew's Top Three Reasons to Visit

1 I held off on this tour until my third visit to Kentucky because I felt like it would be very corporate. That is not the case: there is a nice flow between smaller- and larger-scale production on this tour.

2 The 90 minutes go by quickly. Be prepared, you might get to volunteer to "catch" some Knob Creek in a glass, straight from the barrel.

3 With an eighth generation having its influence felt, there are some interesting things to come for the company, including a step into single malts.

MORE INFORMATION: *www.whiskey-lore.com/jimbeamamerican*

Kentucky Artisan Distillery

ABOUT KENTUCKY ARTISAN DISTILLERY

If you are looking for the official home of Jefferson's Reserve and Jefferson's Ocean At Sea, this is it. Born as a contract distillery in 2012, Kentucky Artisan produces bourbon the old-fashioned way, using pot stills for quantities as small as two barrels. A local operation, they source their grain from Waldeck Farms, just a mile down the road.

Built as a production facility, it can feel a little homemade when you walk through the tour. When I was there, they showed the distilling process through photographs posted on a corkboard. But then, who said the distilling process had to be high tech?

A DirecTV documentary called *Bourbontucky* drew me to Jefferson's Bourbon. It featured the bourbon's creator Trey Zoeller talking about his passion for both history and experimentation. Zoeller's spirit permeates this facility. The tour guides relay the lore surrounding bourbon and the creative techniques used at the distillery. And don't be surprised if you see some historic distilling artifacts during your visit.

LISTEN/WATCH FOR

See if you can spot their unique hand-hammered copper pot still named "The 11." They call this their oldest and most reliable piece of equipment; it has been in use since just after Prohibition.

2020 TASTING EXPERIENCE/KEEPSAKES*

During the tasting, they let us sample three different bourbons: Jefferson's Very Small Batch, Jefferson's Ocean at Sea, and Whiskey Row. We finished the tasting with a sample of their bottled Manhattan cocktail. There were no keepsakes.

GETTING THERE

Kentucky Artisan can be a little tricky to get to. Take Exit 14 off I-71 and head south on Veteran's Memorial Parkway. When you reach State Road 146 in Crestwood, turn left. From there, keep an eye out for Camden Lane. When you reach it, turn left over the railroad track and take another immediate right onto Old Lagrange Road. You will see the distillery on the left. An even better option is to rely on your GPS.

TOUR SCHEDULE

10 a.m.–3 p.m. Mon–Sat; Noon–3 p.m. Sun Hourly, on the hour. Other expanded experiences also available.

SIDE TRIPS

- **Shelby Trails Park & Red Fern Riding Center** - Ready to ride some horses? The riding center can provide you with horses and lessons, or you can even bring your own horse!
- **Yew Dell Botanical Gardens** - If you love gardening and plants, then head next door to see this internationally renowned botanical garden.

CLOSEST DISTILLERIES

- **Old Forester** (SW-19.0 miles)
- **Rabbit Hole** (W-19.2 miles)

At A Glance

FEATURED BRANDS	Jeffersons, Ocean at Sea, Whiskey Row
OWNER	Castle Brands
REGION	Louisville
AVAILABLE TO TOUR	Fermenters, Pot Still, Bottling
COST	$$ - Military discount and children free
LOCATION	36230 Old Lagrange Rd, Crestwood, KY 40014
WEBSITE	*www.kentuckyartisandistillery.com*

Drew's Top Three Reasons to Visit

1 There is a real passion and reverence for history here. The tour will give you an excellent overview of the legends built around the name and character of bourbon.

2 Check out the names of their bourbons: Whiskey Row and Billy Goat Strut are both related to Louisville's rich history.

3 Learning about the aging process of Jefferson's Ocean at Sea will give you an appreciation for the level of creativity employed at this distillery.

MORE INFORMATION: *www.whiskey-lore.com/kentuckyartisan*

ky Peerless Distillery

KENTUCKY PEERLESS DISTILLERY

1881, Peerless Whiskey made its debut in Henderson, Kentucky growing into a successful brand—only to be shut down 40 years later with the onset of Prohibition. But unlike other Prohibition casualties, this distillery revived its fortunes nine decades later, under the guidance of Corky and Carson Taylor. Brought to Louisville in 2014, the reimagined distillery now graces the western end of Whiskey Row.

Kentucky Peerless specializes in small-batch Kentucky Straight Bourbon Whiskey and Kentucky Straight Rye Whiskey, non-chill filtered and bottled at barrel strength. They are one of three distilleries in the state that use a sweet mash process.

When you first walk in the distillery, there is an immediate warm greeting from Rye, the Instagram feline star (follow @ryemeow_) and adopted distillery cat. From there, your guide, maybe even Corky Taylor himself, will regale you with stories of the distillery and family histories. The tour walks you through the distilling process, then into a single story rickhouse, and finishes in their beautiful pub-like tasting room.

LISTEN/WATCH FOR

When the owner, Corky Taylor, went to military school in Tennessee, he had some very famous musical roommates—find out who at the beginning of the tour.

2020 TASTING EXPERIENCE/KEEPSAKES*

At the end of the tour our guide invited us to a tasting of four different whiskeys—three distillery exclusive ryes and a three-year-old small-batch rye whiskey. They included a nice chocolate in the tasting and gave us a uniquely designed tasting glass as a keepsake.

GETTING THERE

If you are downtown already, it is easy to walk down to the western end of Whiskey Row (Main Street). There are also several parking lots in the area; look down Market Street for the best parking opportunities. There is also metered street parking at around $2 per hour.

TOUR SCHEDULE

10:30 a.m.–3:30 p.m Mon–Wed & Sat;
11:30 a.m.–5:30 p.m. Thu–Fri
Hourly, on the half hour. Other expanded experiences also available.

SIDE TRIPS

- **Frazier History Museum** - On the third floor bourbon history comes alive featuring interactive displays, a historic collection of bourbon bottles, and all you need to know to be a bourbon expert.
- **Louisville Riverwalk** - Enjoy a view of the Ohio River and stretch your legs along the walking path.

CLOSEST DISTILLERIES

- **Michter's Fort Nelson Distillery** (SE-0.2 miles)
- **Evan Williams Bourbon Experience** (W-0.4 miles)

At A Glance

FEATURED BRANDS	Peerless
OWNER	Kentucky Peerless Distilling Co.
REGION	Louisville
AVAILABLE TO TOUR	Fermenters, Column Still, Warehouse
COST	$$$ - Veteran and minors discount, children free
LOCATION	120 N 10th St, Louisville, KY 40202
WEBSITE	*www.kentuckypeerless.com*

Drew's Top Three Reasons to Visit

1   This is a great tour if you want to taste cask strength small-batch whiskey. It is a relaxed tasting that includes a chocolate pairing.

2   Kentucky Peerless has a fascinating history that goes back five generations. Listen to the story of Henry Kraver and what happened to all of the leftover whiskey when Prohibition shut the distillery down.

3   Rye may be the most popular and friendly distillery cat in Kentucky.

MORE INFORMATION: *www.whiskey-lore.com/kentuckypeerless*

Limestone Branch Distillery

ABOUT LIMESTONE BRANCH DISTILLERY

Which is the only Kentucky distillery owned by the legendary Beam family? If you said Limestone Branch, then you know your Kentucky bourbon. Part of the seventh generation of Beams, Steve and Paul Beam broke ground on Limestone Branch in 2011. Since then, they have built much of that family history into their tours.

As you check out the family tree in the visitor's center, you will notice another legendary bourbon family name, the Dants. It was J. B. Dant who brought Yellowstone bourbon to market in the 1880s. When the Beam brothers opened the distillery, they partnered with another distiller (LuxCo) to bring this classic name back to the state.

Being a craft distillery, you will see the entire distillation operation consolidated in a single room. The first thing you'll notice is the small bulb-shaped 150-gallon copper pot still. After learning how they distill their product, you get a chance to use a whiskey thief to draw a cask-strength sample from a barrel.

LISTEN/WATCH FOR

In the visitor's center you can see the shovel they used to break ground here in 2011. They also feature some classic bourbon names on the wall, like Early Times, Old Trump, and Yellowstone.

2020 TASTING EXPERIENCE/KEEPSAKES*

After trying some cask-strength whiskey at the shed, they take you into a tasting room with a long bar. Here we sampled expressions of Limestone Branch, Yellowstone, and their sherry cask-finished Minor Case Rye, along with a paired chocolate. I left with a mini Glencairn branded glass as a keepsake.

GETTING THERE

Lebanon is out in the country, so this is more of a destination, rather than a place you stumble upon. That said, it is just down the road from Maker's Mark and pairs beautifully with it, giving you a chance to see both a large-scale operation and a craft distillery. Most likely you will want to use GPS, because the distillery is away from US 68. There is plenty of paved parking outside.

TOUR SCHEDULE

10 a.m.–5 p.m. Mon–Sat; Noon–5 p.m. Sun Hourly, on the hour. Other expanded experiences also available.

SIDE TRIPS

- **Kentucky Cooperage (Independent Stave Company)** - This is one of the coolest parts of the bourbon experience. Learn about different char levels, see the stacks of aging lumber, and experience the craft of barrel making. No cameras inside.

CLOSEST DISTILLERIES

- **Maker's Mark** (N-10.5 miles)
- **Heaven Hill Bourbon Heritage Center** (N-25.6 miles)

At A Glance

FEATURED BRANDS	Limestone Branch, Minor Case, Yellowstone
OWNER	Limestone Branch Distillery
REGION	Bardstown
AVAILABLE TO TOUR	Fermenters, Pot Still, Mini-Warehouse
COST	$ - Military and minors free
LOCATION	1280 Veterans Memorial Hwy, Lebanon, KY 40033
WEBSITE	*www.limestonebranch.com*

Drew's Top Three Reasons to Visit

1 This is a family distillery and they do an excellent job of making you feel a part of it. You may have a chance to meet one of the Beams while you are here.

2 The guides do an excellent job of relating the history of the Beam and Dant families and share some fun anecdotes.

3 If you're planning to head to the Jim Beam American Stillhouse, take a photo of the family tree at Limestone Branch and compare it to the one at Jim Beam. It is fun to see where the common threads are.

MORE INFORMATION: *www.whiskey-lore.com/limestonebranch*

Lux Row Distillery

ABOUT LUX ROW DISTILLERY

While Lux Row may be the new kid in Bardstown, they are no strangers to bourbon. The family-owned company has been in the bourbon industry for over 40 years. And now they have committed to owning their own brands and distilling their own spirits by building a state-of-the-art distillery.

The beautiful country setting gives way to a modern and spacious visitor's center. The tour starts in a theater-style room with a wall-sized promotional video, complete with an inspired soundtrack. From there, you walk into a room with open-top fermenters and mash cookers. Head down the stairs and glance up at the three-story tall column still.

My favorite part of this tour was walking into the fresh new rickhouse. Normally you would expect to experience a heavy dose of angel's share, but here it combines angel's share with fresh wood construction. The fresh wood made it one of the brightest warehouses I have ever been in. The tour finishes in an elegant bar and tasting room.

LISTEN/WATCH FOR

If you are a fan of rock music, find out which whiskey was Rolling Stone Keith Richards' favorite bourbon. And find out about how one of the supporting acts on one of his tours was so inspired by the name of the bourbon that he wrote a song about it.

2020 TASTING EXPERIENCE/KEEPSAKES*

We enjoyed a guided tasting of three whiskeys, paired with three chocolates. There is a nice selection of rye and wheated bourbons including Ezra Brooks, Rebel Yell, and David Nicholson Reserve.

GETTING THERE

The distillery is just outside of Bardstown on the State Road 245 Bypass. If you are using GPS, just be aware that mine sent me down the employee entrance, rather than the visitor entrance. Make sure you are heading to 1 Lux Row. There is plenty of on-site parking.

TOUR SCHEDULE

10 a.m.–3 p.m. Tue–Sat;
11:30 a.m.–3:30 p.m. Sun
Various tours are available.
Hourly, on the hour.

SIDE TRIPS

- **Oscar Getz Museum of Whiskey History** - How did Kentucky survive Prohibition? Who was Carrie Nation? And what did George Washington's still look like? Come see this wonderful collection started by the former owner of Barton 1792. Free.
- **Women's Civil War Museum** - Learn about the roles women played during the American Civil War.

CLOSEST DISTILLERIES

- **Bardstown Bourbon Company** (E-2.9 miles)
- **Heaven Hill Bourbon Heritage Center** (W-3.4 miles)

At A Glance

FEATURED BRANDS	Blood Oath, David Nicholson, Ezra Brooks, Rebel Yell
OWNER	LuxCo
REGION	Bardstown
AVAILABLE TO TOUR	Fermenters, Column Still, Warehouse
COST	$$ - Military and minors free
LOCATION	1 Lux Row, Bardstown, KY 40004
WEBSITE	*www.luxrowdistillers.com*

Drew's Top Three Reasons to Visit

1   I enjoyed the guided tasting here. Where a lot of distilleries give you one chocolate for the tasting experience, Lux Row pairs up three.

2   The campus here is in a nice country setting, on what was once a family farm. The original house looks like it might soon be utilized as an event center.

3   For those interested in seeing what a modern distillery looks like, this is a fresh, new, and well-thought out option.

MORE INFORMATION: *www.whiskey-lore.com/luxrow*

Maker's Mark Distillery

ABOUT MAKER'S MARK DISTILLERY

When I looked to develop a taste for bourbon, I asked someone where I should start. They suggested Maker's Mark. This was no mistake. When Bill Samuels Sr. and his wife Margie bought the historic Burks' Distillery in 1953, their mission was to create a very approachable bourbon. They experimented with a variety of grains until they settled on red winter wheat as a replacement for rye in the mash bill. The resulting bourbon is an excellent starter and has become a staple in homes and taverns.

When planning my first bourbon adventure, Maker's Mark topped my list. What I found was a distillery that had something for everyone. The distillery itself is on the National Register of Historic Places; we sampled sour mash as we viewed the fermentation process; the grounds are picturesque; and fans of Dale Chihuly will enjoy his blown-glass display outside the tasting room.

Before my tour, I was offered a bourbon-flavored coffee. The tour finished with a thorough guided tasting.

LISTEN/WATCH FOR

The tour guide did a nice job of highlighting Bourbon Hall of Fame member Margie Samuels who shares much of the responsibility for the branding of Maker's Mark. Her accomplishments include crafting the Maker's bottle design, the hand dipping of each bottle in red wax, and the Maker's Mark logo.

2020 TASTING EXPERIENCE/KEEPSAKES*

They provided five samples and walked us through each individually. We tried the white dog, Maker's Mark, Maker's 46, Cask Strength, and Private Select. They also provided chocolate at the end of the tasting. As you leave, you can buy a bottle of Maker's Mark from the gift shop and hand dip it yourself. My keepsake was a Maker's Mark label from the print shop.

GETTING THERE

You will definitely need your GPS or an excellent sense of direction, though there is signage once you get close. The distillery is about 30 minutes south of Bardstown and 25 miles northwest of Lebanon, Kentucky. There is plenty of on-site parking.

TOUR SCHEDULE

9:30 a.m.–3:30 p.m. Mon–Sat;
11:30 a.m.–3:30 p.m. Sun
Various tours are available.
No specific schedule.

SIDE TRIPS

- **Abraham Lincoln's Boyhood Home at Knob Creek (National Park Service)**
  See where the 16th President of the United States was born; in the summer, rangers provide guided tours. Free.

CLOSEST DISTILLERIES

- **Limestone Branch Distillery** (SE-7.9 miles)
- **Willett Distillery** (NW-17.4 miles)

At A Glance

FEATURED BRANDS	Maker's Mark
OWNER	Beam Suntory
REGION	Bardstown
AVAILABLE TO TOUR	Fermenters, Print Shop, Warehouse, Bottling
COST	$$ - Veteran and minors discount, active military free
LOCATION	3350 Burks Spring Rd, Loretto, KY 40037
WEBSITE	*www.makersmark.com*

Drew's Top Three Reasons to Visit

1 Located on Star Hill, this historic countryside campus has plenty of photo opportunities including a wagon filled with branded Maker's Mark barrels.

2 The guided tasting is very descriptive and helps you understand how to analyze a whisky while nosing and tasting it.

3 If the term "finishing" confuses you, seeing inside a Maker's Mark 46 barrel with its additional wood staves will clear things up.

MORE INFORMATION: *www.whiskey-lore.com/makersmark*

MB Roland Distillery

ABOUT MB ROLAND DISTILLERY

If you are looking for a distillery with a down-home feeling, MB Roland is an excellent choice. Just north of Clarksville, Tennessee, this veteran-owned distillery was an Amish farm in its previous life. In fact, running electricity to the buildings was one of the first challenges the distillery faced. The 100 gallon still they started production with in 2009 now sits by the front porch of the visitor's center.

One of the first things you will notice is how many spirits they produce using their grain-to-glass philosophy—they are no strangers to experimentation. The distillery makes a variety of moonshines, wheat- and malt-based whiskeys, and they even smoke some of their white corn to create a Dark Fired Kentucky Straight Bourbon.

The tour takes you through the production facility, to the hay barn that stores their aging whiskey, and on to the visitor's center for a leisurely and informative tasting.

LISTEN/WATCH FOR

This is the only distillery I have visited that has square fermenters. Maybe they designed them as space savers or, like Casey Jones Distillery's square coffin stills, maybe they are just easier to load onto a flatbed truck.

2020 TASTING EXPERIENCE/KEEPSAKES*

There is quite the lineup of whiskey and moonshine, and even something called Kentucky Azul. I had my samples split up into seven tastes–they provide you with the best order for tasting. You will also receive a free shot glass. Ask for a State-line pass book and stamp—a quick way to get a nice keepsake by visiting three local distilleries.

GETTING THERE

If you are driving along I-24, head to Exit 89 and turn on State Road 115 toward Pembroke/Oak Grove. The drive for the distillery is about a mile down the road on your right. During busy times, parking in the lot may be a little tight but its country location means that it isn't hard to find other spots where you can park. Watch for cats and dogs.

TOUR SCHEDULE

10 a.m.–5 p.m. Mon–Sat; 1 p.m.–5 p.m. Sun
Various tours are available.
Hourly, on the hour.

SIDE TRIPS

- **Jefferson Davis State Historic Park**
  Check out the obelisk and ride up the elevator. There is also a museum describing Jefferson Davis' life and birthplace.
- **Mammoth Cave National Park**
  Preserved by the National Park Service, this 400-mile chain of caves is the longest in the world. Reserve your spot for the ranger-led tour.

CLOSEST DISTILLERIES

- **Old Glory Distillery (TN)**
  (SE-11.9 miles)
- **Casey Jones Distillery**
  (NW-22.2 miles)

At A Glance

FEATURED BRANDS	MB Roland
OWNER	MB Roland Distillery
REGION	West
AVAILABLE TO TOUR	Fermenters, Pot Still, Warehouse, Bottling
COST	$
LOCATION	137 Barkers Mill Rd, Pembroke, KY 42266
WEBSITE	*www.mbroland.com*

Drew's Top Three Reasons to Visit

1 Animal lovers will enjoy this tour. I met a friendly distillery cat on the way into the visitor's center, and there are several dogs and cats wandering the property.

2 They are the only Kentucky distillery I visited that uses white corn, which is grown and sourced locally.

3 Events are held here that include food trucks and music. Check their website for their main event Pickin' on the Porch.

MORE INFORMATION: *www.whiskey-lore.com/mbroland*

Michter's Fort Nelson Distillery

ABOUT MICHTER'S FORT NELSON DISTILLERY

When you arrive at Michter's Fort Nelson Distillery you will wonder how this beautiful building stood vacant for almost 50 years. Time and the elements almost had their way with this structure, which at one point leaned 22° from its roof to the street. In fact, while touring the facility you may see how they anchored the brick where a seam was forming. Before your tour, watch the video just inside the entrance. This shows you how this wonderful building was brought back to life.

There is very little walking during Michter's standard tour. The focus is on a single floor of production. The tour includes a view of two pot stills and three cypress fermenters. Michter's also uses a cage mill for grinding their grains and there is a short demonstration using a miniature version of the machine.

Michter's has one of the most unusual and well-thought out tasting experiences in Kentucky. You sample several of the scents found in their bourbons before nosing and tasting the product. Michter's also barrels their bourbon at both full strength and a proofed-down version. The effects of this unique barreling style are demonstrated during the tasting. Our tour ended with the choice of personalized cocktails.

LISTEN/WATCH FOR

Michter's may be one of the oldest distilleries in Kentucky, but it didn't start in Kentucky. Learn more about its Pennsylvania heritage while taking the tour.

2020 TASTING EXPERIENCE/KEEPSAKES*

The nosing and tasting presentation is one of the most immersive experiences I've had in Kentucky. We had the three Michter's Single Barrel Rye whiskies, all barrelled at different strengths. Then we tried the Small Batch American Whiskey and Small Batch Bourbon. There were no keepsakes.

GETTING THERE

If you are downtown already, Michter's is in the heart of Whiskey Row (Main Street). There are several parking lots in the area with Market Street featuring several. You will also find street parking at around $2 per hour.

TOUR SCHEDULE

12 a.m.—6 p.m. Mon & Thu–Fri;
11 a.m.–5 p.m. Sat; 1 p.m.–4 p.m. Sun
Various tours are available.
Hourly, on the hour, with exceptions.

SIDE TRIPS

- **The Brown Hotel and Lobby Bar**
  If you love cocktails and history, head into this 1920s hotel and enjoy a drink in the lobby bar to get a dose of nostalgia.
- **Louisville Slugger Museum** - See baseball bats being made, learn the history, and have fun with the interactive exhibits. Perfect for kids.

CLOSEST DISTILLERIES

- **Evan Williams Bourbon Experience** (E-0.2 miles)
- **Kentucky Peerless Distillery** (W-0.3 miles)

At A Glance

FEATURED BRANDS	Michters
OWNER	Chatham Imports
REGION	Louisville
AVAILABLE TO TOUR	Fermenters, Pot Stills
COST	$$$ - Veteran, active military, and minor discounts
LOCATION	801 W Main St, Louisville, KY 40202
WEBSITE	*www.michters.com*

Drew's Top Three Reasons to Visit

1 The multi-sensory tour is a creative way for beginners to get a sense of the smells they will experience in bourbon.

2 Michter's is one of the few distilleries that proofs their whiskey down to near 100 proof before it enters the barrel. You can taste the effects of this technique at the end of the tour.

3 It was nice to finish up the tour with a personalized cocktail.

MORE INFORMATION: *www.whiskey-lore.com/michters*

Neeley Family Distillery

ABOUT NEELEY FAMILY DISTILLERY

The history of moonshine is an integral part of Kentucky history. The battles fought behind the scenes were life altering and you will see much of that history during your visit to Neeley Family Distillery. It's also fascinating to learn that this lesser-known distillery features the longest lineage of any distillery in Kentucky—stretching back 11 generations to Ireland.

Neeley brings this distilling experience to both bourbon and moonshine. They blaze their own trail in three ways. First, they use the triple-pot distilling technique used by their Irish forefathers. Second, they rely heavily on wild yeast. And third, they are one of only three distilleries in the state of Kentucky to embrace the sweet mash process.

The tour begins with a rousing video, before walking you through the entire process and ending with a choice of moonshines and bourbons.

LISTEN/WATCH FOR

Neeley is a large proponent of using wild yeast strains. One of the first tour stops is to see the pot where they store their wild yeast. And while newer distilleries are opting for closed fermenters, Neeley uses a mix of stainless-steel and wooden open-topped fermenters that attract wild yeast.

2020 TASTING EXPERIENCE/KEEPSAKES*

They have a wide selection of moonshines and some young bourbons. You will get several samples during your tasting. The bourbon was flavorful, and has won awards in the young bourbon category. There were no keepsakes on my visit.

GETTING THERE

Take Exit 55 off I-71, between Louisville and Cincinnati. Head north and look for the Kentucky Speedway sign. Turn right and the distillery is located immediately on the left.

TOUR SCHEDULE

10 a.m.–5 p.m. Mon–Sat; Noon–5 p.m. Sun Hourly, on the hour. Other expanded experiences also available.

SIDE TRIPS

- **Dirty Turtle Offroad Park** - If you want to adventure off-road in your own vehicle, check out the Dirty Turtle's wide range of trails.
- **Kentucky Speedway** - Every July, the thunder of NASCAR invades the Bluegrass State at this fan-friendly stock car racetrack.

CLOSEST DISTILLERIES

- **Boone County Distillery** (NE-30.4 miles)
- **Kentucky Artisan Distillery** (SW-41.9 miles)

At A Glance

FEATURED BRANDS	Neeley Family Distilling
OWNER	Neeley Family Distilling
REGION	North
AVAILABLE TO TOUR	Fermenters, Pot Still, Warehouse, Bottling
COST	$$
LOCATION	4360 Ky Highway 1130, Sparta, KY 41083
WEBSITE	*www.neeleyfamilydistillery.com*

Drew's Top Three Reasons to Visit

1 Everyone I talked to was a member of the family. So this is about as "family" as a distillery gets.

2 Do you love action-adventure movies? Are you a fan of the Discovery Channel show *Moonshiners*? The introductory video and tale by owner and master distiller Royce Neeley will be right up your alley. I will warn you though, it is at least a PG-13 endeavor.

3 Arrive early and check out the amazing family history collected in the visitor's center, including Royce's pot still that was confiscated by his father while the soon-to-be master distiller was attending the University of Kentucky.

MORE INFORMATION: *www.whiskey-lore.com/neeleyfamily*

New Riff Distillery

ABOUT NEW RIFF DISTILLERY

After 25 years of owning a party store, founder Ken Lewis decided to make his mark in the Kentucky bourbon industry. So, along with his co-founder Jay Erisman, he built a distillery right next to the party store. The New Riff Distillery sits directly across the Ohio River from Cincinnati.

I must admit, their beautifully statuesque bottles and branding were the initial inspiration for my visit. But once on-site their passion for quality and breaking new ground took center stage. Their attention to detail reaches all the way to the quality of the beer they create for the distillation process. The whiskey is non-chill filtered and follows Bottled-in-Bond standards.

The tour travels through the entire distillation process. As you climb and descend the stairs, you view fermentation and milling, and work your neck muscles checking out the three-story column still. We had a sample of their 135 proof high rye bourbon right off the still and tasted the 100 proof and single-barrel expressions at the guided tasting.

LISTEN/WATCH FOR

Be careful where you park. I'm just kidding. But you'll get my meaning when you see the location of their well water source.

2020 TASTING EXPERIENCE/KEEPSAKES*

They gave us the opportunity to taste up to four expressions. Our choices were the Bottled-in-Bond and single-barrel versions of their Kentucky Straight Bourbon and Kentucky Straight Rye. They also offered samples of their Kentucky Wild Gin—one of which is barrel finished. There were no keepsakes, but they gave us a wooden nickel to turn in for $10 off a bottle of spirits. My grandmother would be upset if I took a wooden nickel, so I traded it in.

GETTING THERE

If you are coming up I-75 from the south, GPS will lead you into Ohio before coming back into Kentucky to reach the distillery. If it is rush hour this might be a problem, but it was a very easy drive for me on a Saturday. It is right off of the exit and New Riff shares a large parking lot with the Party Source.

TOUR SCHEDULE

Noon–4 p.m. Tue–Sat; Noon–3 p.m. Sun
Various tours are available.
Hourly, on the hour.

SIDE TRIPS

- **BB Riverboats** - Ever thought of riding a riverboat or doing a riverboat dinner cruise? Here you can find a variety of experiences, from lunch and dinner cruises to entertainment for the kids.
- **Newport Aquarium** - Penguins. Need I say more? Well, there is a lot more. Those who love sea life can enjoy viewing a wide range of exhibits including stingrays, sharks, and more.

CLOSEST DISTILLERIES

- **Second Sight Distillery** (W-5.5 miles)
- **Boone County Distilling** (NW-18.3 miles)

At A Glance

FEATURED BRANDS	New Riff
OWNER	New Riff Distilling
REGION	North
AVAILABLE TO TOUR	Milling, Fermenting, Column Still
COST	$$ - Minors free
LOCATION	24 Distillery Way Newport, KY 41073
WEBSITE	*www.newriffdistilling.com*

Drew's Top Three Reasons to Visit

1 They have some experimental grains they are working with, including beer-friendly chocolate stout and IPA.

2 They hired master brewer Brian Sprance to be their head distiller. Most distilleries tell you to not judge their bourbon by the beer, but New Riff is proud of the beer they produce for distillation.

3 If you like rye, they make a high rye bourbon and a rye whiskey. At the time of writing they were only in their sixth year; look for an older age statement whiskey in the next few years.

MORE INFORMATION: *www.whiskey-lore.com/newriff*

Old Forester Distillery

ABOUT OLD FORESTER DISTILLERY

In 2018, Louisville's Whiskey Row welcomed Old Forester Distillery back to its original location. But don't let the building's slim profile, or its downtown location fool you. This is a complete distillery experience—one of the most complete in Kentucky—and includes the only on-site cooperage in the entire state.

The Old Forester brand and its solid reputation date back to 1870, when a medical supply salesman began rectifying whiskey and made this the first whiskey to be sold in sealed bottles. George Garvin Brown was a pioneer in the bourbon industry and his exploits are well covered during the tour, including his fight against Prohibition.

If you can swing it, plan your tour sometime between Tuesday and Saturday to see the distillery in full operation. If the cooperage is in production, you might even see a barrel shaped and fired before your eyes. There is also a chance you will see the bottling process. The tour finishes with a guided tasting. By the way, if you hear a drum banging out front around noon, you can watch as barrels of whiskey are rolled up onto a flatbed truck.

LISTEN/WATCH FOR

Look for the old advertisements on the wall—you'll spot the original spelling of Old Forester.

2020 TASTING EXPERIENCE/KEEPSAKES*

When I toured, we tasted three selections including Old Forester 86 Proof, States-man, and Old Forester 100 Proof. They also paired a chocolate with the tasting. There were no keepsakes.

GETTING THERE

If you are downtown already, it is an easy walk down to the eastern end of Whiskey Row (Main Street) to reach the distillery. There are several parking lots in the area. Look down Main Street's south side for the most parking lot opportunities. Metered street parking is also available at around $2 per hour.

TOUR SCHEDULE

10 a.m.–6 p.m. Tue–Thu;
10 a.m.–7 p.m. Fri & Sat; Noon–5 p.m. Sun
Tours every 15 minutes. Note that the distillery is not producing whiskey on Sunday or Monday, but is still open for tours. Other expanded experiences are also available.

SIDE TRIPS

- **Doc Crow's Southern Smokehouse & Raw Bar** - Take some time out for a meal here and sample their amazing selection of whiskey. Their half pours are perfect for supplementing your day of tasting.
- **KFC Yum! Center** - After a day of bourbon tours, head to downtown Louisville for some Louisville Cardinal basketball or to see a concert.

CLOSEST DISTILLERIES

- **Evan Williams Bourbon Experience** (W-0.4 miles)
- **Jim Beam Urban Stillhouse** (SW-0.5 miles)

At A Glance

FEATURED BRANDS	Old Forester
OWNER	Brown-Forman
REGION	Louisville
AVAILABLE TO TOUR	Fermenters, Column Still, Cooperage, Warehouse, Bottling
COST	$$ - Military and minor discount
LOCATION	119 W Main St, Louisville, KY 40202
WEBSITE	*www.oldforester.com*

Drew's Top Three Reasons to Visit

1   The on-site cooperage is a treat. If you can't make it to Kentucky Cooperage, this is a great opportunity to see them shape, bind, and fire a barrel right before your eyes.

2   This is an extremely visual tour; ideal if you learn best through pictures.

3   It is great to see the bourbon industry treasuring its heritage. Look for pictures of what this distillery looked like in the 19th century. Also note the medicinal use advertisement that suggests longer life can be achieved by drinking this whiskey.

MORE INFORMATION: *www.whiskey-lore.com/oldforester*

Preservation Distillery

ABOUT PRESERVATION DISTILLERY

One day a contract distiller was driving through Bardstown, Kentucky when she happened upon a farm, tobacco barn, and local entertainment venue known as Hillbilly Heaven. Having a long-time dream of creating her own spirits, Marci Palatella purchased the property and Preservation Distillery was born in 2014.

The first thing you will notice when entering the production facility is how they have fit a distillery into a pre-existing barn without the need of radical alterations to its outer dimensions. Their water source is from an on-site well that drills below a bed of limestone, while their grains all come from a farm right down the road in New Haven.

At the time of writing, Preservation had not officially released their bourbon, but you can sample a young version of it during the tour. The other products you will sample are bourbons sourced by the owner.

LISTEN/WATCH FOR

This is a working farm and distillery. Look to the right as you drive down the road into the distillery and you'll spot their longhorn cattle. Their future plans include growing many of the grains used on the farm itself.

2020 TASTING EXPERIENCE/KEEPSAKE

Our tasting included four spirits. We h the Cowboy Little Barrel Blended Whisk Wattie Boone 7 Year, and Rare Perfecti 14 Year. These are all sourced. They al gave us a sample of the bourbon they a producing on-site. To cleanse our pala between tastings, we received a bag caramel-coated popcorn. There were keepsakes.

GETTING THERE

Easy to access, you will find Preservati Distillery just off of the Martha Lay Collins Bluegrass Parkway at the US 3 exit, south of Bardstown. It has a gra parking lot with plenty of room for vi tors, even during events.

TOUR SCHEDULE

1 p.m.–4 p.m. Tue–Thu;
10 a.m.–4 p.m. Fri & Sat
Various tours are available.
Hourly, on the hour.

SIDE TRIPS

- **McIntyre's Winery and Berries** - En an excellent selection of fruity wines tasting.
- **Old Bardstown Village & Civil W Museum** - Experience the beginnir of Bardstown and learn of its impact the Civil War.

CLOSEST DISTILLERIES

- **Barton 1792 Distillery** (N-2.5 miles)
- **Willett Distillery** (E-3.2 miles)

At A Glance

FEATURED BRANDS	Cowboy Little Barrel, Very Old St. Nick, Wattie Boone & Sons
OWNER	Preservation Distillery
REGION	Bardstown
AVAILABLE TO TOUR	Milling, Fermenters, Column Still
COST	$$ - Military and minor discount
LOCATION	426 Sutherland Rd, Bardstown, KY 40004
WEBSITE	*www.preservationdistillery.com*

Drew's Top Three Reasons to Visit

1 There is a wonderful trend toward sustainable practices in the bourbon industry. Small craft distilleries like Preservation are making a commitment to these practices and creating a blueprint for the entire industry.

2 Seeing how they have used every inch of the barn is worth the price of admission. They even do their own milling within its small confines.

3 If you are planning a wedding or event and want to host it in the Bourbon Capital of the World, be sure to check out this former home of Hillbilly Heaven.

MORE INFORMATION: *www.whiskey-lore.com/preservation*

Rabbit Hole Distillery

ABOUT RABBIT HOLE DISTILLERY

If I had to describe this urban distillery, I would call it modern and industrial chic. To me, the production area feels like you are walking into an ERECTOR Set or, even better, the lair of one of James Bond's villains.

Founder Kaveh Zamanian built a facility with transparency in mind. It is a tourist-friendly facility that will amaze you with what they can accomplish in such a small footprint and with some creative imagination.

You start the tour with a taste of bourbon in their beautifully designed gift shop and visitor's center. As you enjoy your sample the tour makes its way past a series of windows and visual displays that show the bourbon-making process. A ride up the elevator takes you to the vertically designed production facility. The tour finishes at the top of their tall column still. From here, you make your way into a cocktail bar, tasting room, and event space with its magnificent view of downtown Louisville.

LISTEN/WATCH FOR

Rabbit Hole recently rebranded their product line with names that celebrate Louisville and its history. Listen for the backstory on names like Heigold, Cavehill, Boxergrail, and Wool and Water.

2020 TASTING EXPERIENCE/KEEPSAKE

During our tour, there was an event goi on in the cocktail bar, so we did our ta ing in the gift shop on the first floor. ' enjoyed a sampling of Rabbit Hole's whe ed Kentucky Straight Bourbon, Kentuc Straight Rye, a PX sherry cask-finisł straight bourbon whiskey, and a Lond Dry Gin finished in rye barrels. The were no keepsakes.

GETTING THERE

The distillery is just over a mile away fro the eastern end of Whiskey Row, so wa ing from downtown will take time. If y want to avoid the long walk, they ha their own parking and there is plenty street parking in front of Rabbit Hole East Jefferson Street.

TOUR SCHEDULE

Noon–6 p.m. Tue--Thu;
11 a.m.–7 p.m. Fri & Sat; 1–6 p.m. Sun
Various tours are available.
No specific schedule

SIDE TRIPS

- **The Silver Dollar** - A modern juke jo featuring a wide selection of bourb fun music, and tasty working-cl southern dishes.
- **Thomas Edison House** - See one the homes where the famous inven Thomas Edison lived; some of his inv tions are on display.

CLOSEST DISTILLERIES

- **Angel's Envy Distillery** (NW-0.3 mile
- **Old Forester Distillery** (W-0.9 miles)

At A Glance

FEATURED BRANDS	Rabbit Hole
OWNER	Pernod Ricard
REGION	Louisville
AVAILABLE TO TOUR	Fermentation, Lab, Column Still
COST	$$$ - Military, minors and senior discounts
LOCATION	711 E Jefferson St, Louisville, KY 40202
WEBSITE	*www.rabbitholedistillery.com*

Drew's Top Three Reasons to Visit

1 There is a lot of modern beauty in the building's design; I have not seen another distillery like it. Even the two-paneled awning out front shows a creative edge.

2 In the summer, the distillery offers outdoor seating. But the best spot for enjoying a dram is on the third floor, looking out at downtown.

3 They use a grain-to-glass philosophy, meaning their spirits are not sourced. So even though they are new, Rabbit Hole produces all the spirits you taste.

MORE INFORMATION: *www.whiskey-lore.com/rabbithole*

Stitzel-Weller

ABOUT STITZEL-WELLER

If you are planning to take in three or four tours when you come to Kentucky, then you will find Stitzel-Weller a nice change of pace from the tours that focus on process. Here, you can learn how A. Ph. Stitzel and W. L. Weller survived Prohibition by selling medicinal whiskey. You may also hear about how Julian "Pappy" Van Winkle, Sr. helped get the distillery back on its feet after Prohibition.

Many famous brands, including Pappy Van Winkle, Rebel Yell, Old Fitzgerald, and W. L. Weller, were once distilled here. However, it has not been a functioning distillery since 1992 so they use it for its rickhouse space and to honor its historical significance.

When you arrive, check in at the security gate. Once inside the visitor's center and gift shop, you can enjoy a cup of coffee or purchase a cocktail. The tour guide gives a brief overview of the bourbon-making process before taking you into a historic warehouse. You get a chance to view the barrel-repair cooperage and the tour finishes back at the visitor's center with a guided tasting.

LISTEN/WATCH FOR

If you are into collectables, listen for details about Blade and Bow's Five Key Club. Keys found on bottles of Blade and Bow can lead to recognition by Stitzel-Weller.

2020 TASTING EXPERIENCE/KEEPSAKE

They gave us four tastes including Bul 10 year, Blade and Bow, I.W. Harper a Bulleit Rye. There was also a nice tast notes sheet provided so that we could r each whiskey. There were no keepsakes

GETTING THERE

This is a great distillery experience to v if you are in the southern part of Louisv or heading to Churchill Downs. The dis ery is just off of US 31W, about 15 minu south of downtown Louisville. Once y get through the security gate, there is pl ty of parking. The visitor's center entra is on the side of the building.

TOUR SCHEDULE

11 a.m.–3 p.m. Mon, Wed & Thu;
10 a.m.–3 p.m. Fri & Sat; 1–3 p.m. Sun
No specific schedule. Other expanded experiences also available.

SIDE TRIPS

- **Kentucky Derby Museum and Ch chill Downs** - Experience the history this iconic horse-racing track and to the facilities – or stay for a race!
- **Speed Art Museum** - Check out ultra-modern design and exhibits of t Kentucky art museum.

CLOSEST DISTILLERIES

- **Jim Beam Urban Stillhouse** (N-5.5 miles)
- **Kentucky Peerless Distillery** (N-5.5 miles)

At A Glance

FEATURED BRANDS	Blade and Bow, Bulleit, I.W. Harper
OWNER	Diageo
REGION	Louisville
AVAILABLE TO TOUR	Warehouse
COST	$$$ - Military and minors free
LOCATION	3860 Fitzgerald Rd, Shively, KY 40216
WEBSITE	*www.bulleit.com*

Drew's Top Three Reasons to Visit

1 If you are lucky, when you arrive at the security gate you will get to meet Perry. He has worked for Stitzel-Weller for over 50 years and provides a warm greeting.

2 I have heard from several people that the tour guides are top notch. On my tour, our guide disclosed that she was only finishing her third day. I could hardly believe it—she did an excellent job with the whiskey tasting and in providing the history of the distillery.

3 The guided tasting comes with a tasting notes scorecard, which gives you the ability to remember your tasting notes, long after your tasting experience. This is a great tool if you want to grow your bourbon-tasting abilities.

MORE INFORMATION: *www.whiskey-lore.com/stitzelweller*

Town Branch Distillery

ABOUT TOWN BRANCH DISTILLERY

Experience a little of the old country at this distillery and brewery combination on the edge of downtown Lexington. Founded by Irishman Pearse Lyons—whose name also graces a distillery in Dublin—this is one of the few Kentucky distilleries that produces a single malt whiskey in the Scottish tradition.

The tour starts with a video that introduces Lexington's brewing heritage. It also includes the late Pearse Lyons talking about his vision for the distillery and the birth of their bourbon-barrel-aged Kentucky Ale.

As the walking portion of the tour begins, the guide takes you to the brewery and then the beer tasting room. After the beer samples, the tour continues across the street in the distillery. The main room features two wooden washbacks and two beautiful Forsyth Pot Stills from Speyside, Scotland. They also have a spirit safe, which is a legal requirement in scotch distilleries. After learning their process for making whiskey, the tour finishes with a tasting of their spirits.

LISTEN/WATCH FOR

Barrels get a workout in this distillery and brewhouse. Listen how the barrels go through uses between bourbon, beer, and their single malt whiskey.

2020 TASTING EXPERIENCE/KEEPSAKE

The tasting here is unique. They give y[...] four tokens and give you seven beers a[...] seven spirits to choose from. I used o[...] token on beer and the remaining three [...] spirits. We also received an extra taste [...] their Bluegrass Sundown liqueur. The[...] were no keepsakes.

GETTING THERE

This is down the road from Rupp Are[...] in Downtown Lexington. There is a pa[...] ing lot behind the distillery and plenty [...] parking along the road. If you are stay[...] downtown, it is very easy to walk to a[...] there is a historic neighborhood in-b[...] tween.

TOUR SCHEDULE

10 a.m.–4 p.m. Mon–Wed**;
10 a.m.–6 p.m. Thu–Sat; Noon–4 p.m. Su[...] Various tours are available. Hourly, on t[...] hour. Hours vary and during the win[...] they may be closed on Tuesdays a[...] Wednesdays.

SIDE TRIPS

- **Mary Todd Lincoln House** - The ho[...] of the First Lady is available to tour [...] a fee. Closed during the winter month[...]
- **Rupp Arena** - Home of the Univer[...] ty of Kentucky Wildcats, also host[...] concerts, and family events.

CLOSEST DISTILLERIES

- **Barrel House Distilling** (N-1.9 miles)
- **James E. Pepper Distilling** (N-1.9 mil[...]

At A Glance

FEATURED BRANDS	Pearse Lyons Reserve, Town Branch
OWNER	AllTech
REGION	Lexington
AVAILABLE TO TOUR	Brewery, Fermenter, Pot Still, Bottling
COST	$$ - Military and senior discounts, minors free
LOCATION	420 Cross St, Lexington, KY 40508
WEBSITE	*www.lexingtonbrewingco.com*

Drew's Top Three Reasons to Visit

1 It is also the only distillery in Kentucky that integrates a brewery.

2 If you want to see how they make whisky in Scotland without heading overseas, this will give you a nice review.

3 During the tasting, you can choose from several whiskeys, including Irish Whiskey from Pearse Lyons in Dublin.

MORE INFORMATION: *www.whiskey-lore.com/townbranch*

Wilderness Trail Distillery

ABOUT WILDERNESS TRAIL DISTILLERY

Are you ready to geek out on bourbon? If so, Wilderness Trail is the distillery to lead you through the science of whiskey. Not only do they distill their own bourbon, rye, vodka, and rum, they also provide storage, production, testing, and scientific evaluation for other distilleries.

With this strong background, it should come as no surprise the tour starts with the laboratory. Here they give you a sense of their standing as scientific problem solvers. The tour continues up a flight of stairs where you see the sweet mash process in action. Heading back downstairs they explain the distillation process as you view their hybrid pot and column stills. On my tour, we sampled 136 proof rye right off the still and finished the tour with a guided tasting in their visitor's center.

This is an excellent change of pace tour and a first-rate option for those who want an understanding of the process. Be aware that the distillery closes at lunchtime for an hour.

LISTEN/WATCH FOR

Learn about the multiple ways copper stills benefit the whiskey making process. Also notice the Vendome stills; located in Louisville, they are the standard for distilleries across Kentucky.

2020 TASTING EXPERIENCE/KEEPSAKES*

Our tasting included four selections: Wilderness Trail Straight Kentucky Bourbon, Kentucky Straight Rye Whiskey, Blue Heron Vodka, and Harvest Rum. They make these spirits on-site. We received a Wilderness Trail shot glass as a keepsake.

GETTING THERE

It is advisable to program your GPS for the drive here. The distillery is southwest of Lexington and just west of Danville—just down State Road 34. The parking lot provides plenty of space for vehicles.

TOUR SCHEDULE

10 a.m.–4 p.m. Tue–Sat;
11:30 a.m.–3:30 p.m. Sun
Hourly, but closed for lunch. Gift Shop open until 5 p.m. Tue–Sat for tastings.

SIDE TRIPS

- **Great American Dollhouse Museum**
  The social history of the United States being told in miniature. This museum contains over 200 dollhouses.
- **Perryville Battlefield State Park**
  Kentucky was a border state during the Civil War and critical to whichever side won her over. View the site of the Confederate advance into Kentucky.

CLOSEST DISTILLERIES

- **Limestone Branch Distillery**
  (W-26.8 miles)
- **Four Roses Distillery** (N-29.2 miles)

At A Glance

FEATURED BRANDS	Wilderness Trail
OWNER	Wilderness Trail Distillery
REGION	Central
AVAILABLE TO TOUR	Lab, Fermentation, Column Stills, Hybrid Pot Still
COST	$
LOCATION	4095 Lebanon Rd, Danville, KY 40422
WEBSITE	*www.wildernesstraildistillery.com*

Drew's Top Three Reasons to Visit

1 Wilderness Trail's lab is a trusted facility for troubleshooting issues across Kentucky's bourbon industry. It's definitely worth a view.

2 All of this focus on science yields some excellent spirits. However, they aren't too much in the head to get to the heart of what makes a whiskey great.

3 Since my visit, they have opened a brand new visitor's center complete with a cocktail bar, gift shop, and lounge.

MORE INFORMATION: *www.whiskey-lore.com/wildernesstrail*

Wild Turkey Distillery

ABOUT WILD TURKEY DISTILLERY

Wild Turkey has been a staple in bars and American whiskey shops since Austin Nichols named it in 1942. It is also a cultural icon, having been featured in several movies and television shows including *NCIS*, *Fear and Loathing in Las Vegas*, and *Thelma and Louise*.

Under the stewardship of master distiller Jimmy Russell, the brand has grown to include a barrel proof whiskey called Rare Breed, Longbranch, and the distiller's namesake Russell's Reserve bourbon and rye whiskey. They are produced and bottled in a large production facility surrounded by several warehouses in Lawrenceburg, Kentucky.

Because of the campus size, a bus will take you to the production facility. You will climb stairs to reach the huge fermentation room that features the Wild Turkey lab and a huge column still. Next, the bus takes you to a whiskey warehouse, where you get to smell the angel's share firsthand. The tour finishes with a guided tasting and a beautiful view of the Kentucky River.

LISTEN/WATCH FOR

I've heard that legendary distiller Jimmy Russell pops into the visitor's center and greets guests from time to time. That would be a real treat—this is most likely on a weekday.

2020 TASTING EXPERIENCE/KEEPSAKES*

Our tasting went beyond the flagship product and highlighted the elevated Russell Reserve Rye, Russell Reserve Bourbon, and Rare Breed. They also threw in a taste of American Honey Stinger, which is a flavored whiskey. There were no keepsakes—unless you are lucky enough to get Jimmy's autograph.

GETTING THERE

From Lexington, just head out US 60 to Versailles and then turn onto US 62. From Frankfort, it is better to head through Lawrenceburg. Parking is limited, so arrive early enough for your tour to get a space on busy days.

TOUR SCHEDULE

9 a.m.–4 p.m. Mon–Sat;
11 a.m.–3 p.m. Sun (Mar–Dec only)
Hourly, on the hour. The visitor's center is open until 5 p.m. with a cocktail bar and view.

SIDE TRIPS

- **Rising Sons Home Farm Winery**
  A family owned winery featuring wine tastings and homemade jams.
- **WinStar Farm** - Seasonal tours of the stallion barn, breeding shed, and a drive around this working horse farm.

CLOSEST DISTILLERIES

- **Four Roses Distillery** (SW-7.8 miles)
- **Woodford Reserve Distillery** (N-11.3 miles)

At A Glance

FEATURED BRANDS	Longbranch, Russell's Reserve, Wild Turkey
OWNER	Campari America
REGION	Central
AVAILABLE TO TOUR	Fermentation, Lab, Column Still, Warehouse
COST	$$ - Military and minors free
LOCATION	1417 Versailles Rd, Lawrenceburg, KY 40342
WEBSITE	*www.wildturkeybourbon.com*

Drew's Top Three Reasons to Visit

1 If you have been doing craft distillery tours, or even some majors, this is the ideal tour for demonstrating what large-scale production looks like.

2 The tasting takes place in a nice environment, with part of a copper still used for displaying your tasting selection.

3 Take in the magnificent view of the Jo Blackburn Bridge and Kentucky River from the cocktail bar and tasting room.

MORE INFORMATION: *www.whiskey-lore.com/wildturkey*

Willett Distillery

ABOUT WILLETT DISTILLERY

The Willett name has roots all the way back to the early days of Nelson County and Kentucky bourbon. In fact, this property and Warehouse A were in use in 1937, just after Prohibition. But ownership and visions changed over the years and it wasn't until 2012 that the current distillery re-emerged under the leadership of Kentucky Bourbon Hall of Famer Even Kulsveen and his wife Martha Harriett Willett Kulsveen.

Over the last few years, Willett has built a solid reputation for producing high quality bourbon and rye whiskeys. They make six different bourbons utilizing six individual mash bills.

The tour visits the beautiful stone and wood distillery. There is plenty of family history, process and distilling philosophy during the tour. After a trip to the warehouse, the tour concludes in the visitor's center with a wide selection of bourbons to taste. There is also a bar and restaurant on-site.

LISTEN/WATCH FOR

This was the first distillery I visited where I saw a distillery cat. Sometimes distill-eries brought in cats to kill the rodents that ate the milled grains, and other times feral cats would adopt a distillery. Since there are very few distilleries that still mill their own grains, distillery cats have now evolved into Instagram stars.

2020 TASTING EXPERIENCE/KEEPSAKES*

We began our tasting by having nine different spirits described to us. Of those, we could pick out three to taste. I wanted to try the higher proof bourbons, but I had also planned my next tour a little too close to this one. If you want to taste their best and tour another distillery, plan a little extra time between both. The full-size Willett branded Glencairn whiskey glass provided for the tasting was ours to take as a keepsake.

GETTING THERE

Your GPS should bring you to this distillery without too much trouble. It is just south of Heaven Hill Bourbon Heritage Center on Loretto Road. The entrance comes up quickly on the left, so be prepared. Also, this distillery has a gravel path that zigzags to the parking lot.

TOUR SCHEDULE

10 a.m.–3 p.m. Mon–Wed;
10 a.m.–4 p.m. Thu–Sat
Various tours are available. Tours hourly. Seasonal schedule may vary.

SIDE TRIPS

- **Basilica of Saint Joseph Proto-Cathedral** - One of the four original dioceses in the United States, this historic cathedral is a nod to Bardstown's Catholic roots.

CLOSEST DISTILLERIES

- **Heaven Hill Bourbon Heritage Center** (N-1.3 miles)
- **Barton 1792 Distillery** (NW-3.4 miles)

At A Glance

FEATURED BRANDS	Johnny Drum, Kentucky Pure, Kentucky Vintage, Noah's Mill, Rowan's Creek, Willett Pot Still Reserve
OWNER	Kentucky Bourbon Distillers
REGION	Bardstown
AVAILABLE TO TOUR	Fermenters, Pot Still, Warehouse
COST	$$$ - Minors free, American Heroes Discount
LOCATION	1869 Loretto Rd, Bardstown, KY 40004
WEBSITE	*www.willettdistillery.com*

Drew's Top Three Reasons to Visit

1 Willett's uses a long-necked copper pot still for its distillation. It is a beauty to behold. The Willett Pot Still Reserve's bottle represents the shape of this graceful whiskey production vessel.

2 Unlike some distilleries that get you focused on certain expressions, at Willett you can choose three tastes from any of the nine bottles offered.

3 When it is open, stop by the bar at Willett's for some small-plate tastings and cocktails.

MORE INFORMATION: *www.whiskey-lore.com/willett*

Woodford Reserve Distillery

ABOUT WOODFORD RESERVE DISTILLERY

If you are looking for a distillery dripping with bourbon history, Woodford Reserve will fit the bill. Starting its life as the Old Oscar Pepper Distillery in 1838, one of its first employees was Scottish chemist Dr. James C. Crow. The stocks of Old Crow he produced here in the first half of the 19th century became legendary for their quality. The main part of the distillery dates back to those early days.

The tour starts in the visitor's center and moves by bus to the main distillery. It may depend on your particular guide, but we had one of the most thorough and easy to understand presentations of the distillation process anywhere in Kentucky. Add to that the pristine nature of the distillery, the beautiful campus, and the triple pot stills, and Woodford Reserve is a jewel.

After stepping through the production facility, you have time to smell the angel's share in one of their historic warehouses. The tour concludes in the visitor's center with a guided tasting and chocolate pairing.

LISTEN/WATCH FOR

Notice the three pot stills sitting side by side. This might lead some to conclude that Woodford Reserve's bourbon is triple pot distilled. It is, however, a bit more complicated. Listen as they describe their process.

2020 TASTING EXPERIENCE/KEEPSAKES*

They gave us three bourbons to taste: Woodford Reserve Distiller's Select, Woodford Reserve Rye and Woodford Reserve Double Oaked, paired with a walnut-topped piece of chocolate. They show you a flavor wheel and walk you through the tasting process. There were no keepsakes.

GETTING THERE

There are two different ways to get to Woodford Reserve and it is best to use your GPS. Use caution coming in from either direction: the road can be narrow and there are several blind hills and curves. Coming from the south you will see plenty of wonderful horse farms and pastures, so it is very easy to get distracted.

TOUR SCHEDULE

10 a.m.–3 p.m. Mon–Sat; 1 p.m.–3 p.m. Sun Various tours are available. Seasonal schedule may vary.

SIDE TRIPS

Sun Valley Farm - As you drive to the distillery, you will see a variety of horse farms along the way. This family farm provides tours.

CLOSEST DISTILLERIES

- **Castle & Key Distillery** (NW-3.3 miles)
- **Glenns Creek Distillery** (NW-4.2 miles)

At A Glance

FEATURED BRANDS	Woodford Reserve
OWNER	Brown-Forman
REGION	Central
AVAILABLE TO TOUR	Fermenters, Pot Stills, Warehouse
COST	$$$ - Minors and veterans discounts
LOCATION	7785 McCracken Pike, Versailles, KY 40383
WEBSITE	*www.woodfordreserve.com*

Drew's Top Three Reasons to Visit

1 Woodford Reserve is brilliantly maintained and has a rich tradition—perfect for history lovers. The beautiful production area sits on the National Register of Historic Places as the "Labrot & Graham Distillery." Its original name (in 1838) was the Old Oscar Pepper Distillery. However, the origins of distilling on this site go all the way back to Elijah Pepper in 1812.

2 They had one of the best descriptions of the whiskey making process in Kentucky, making it an excellent choice for first timers.

3 The three beautiful pot stills make for a wonderful (Instagrammable) photo.

MORE INFORMATION: *www.whiskey-lore.com/woodfordreserve*

Other Distilleries (By Region)

Bardstown

BOUNDARY OAK DISTILLERY ($)

Boundary Oak Distillery LLC
www.boundaryoakdistillery.com
2000 Boundary Oak Dr,
Radcliff, KY 40160
Brand: Kentucky Amber

FOUR ROSES BOTTLING FACILITY ($)

Kirin
www.fourrosesbourbon.com
624 Lotus Rd,
Coxs Creek, KY 40013
Brand: Four Roses

KENTUCKY OWL

SPI Group/Bardstown
www.kentuckyowlbourbon.com
Brand: Kentucky Owl

Central

SIX MILE CREEK DISTILLERY (N/A)

Patriot Brands LLC/Central
www.sixmilecreekdistillery.com
12606 Castle Hwy,
Pleasureville, KY 40057
Brand: Six Mile Creek

THREE BOYS FARM DISTILLERY ($$)

Whiskey Thief Distilling
Company Inc/Central
www.threeboysfarmdistillery.com
283 Crab Orchard Rd,
Frankfort, KY 40601
Brands: Three Boys, Whiskey Thief

Lexington

BARREL HOUSE DISTILLING CO ($)

Woodshed Beverage LLC
www.barrelhousedistillery.com
1200 Manchester St,
Lexington, KY 40504
Brands: Barrel House, Rockcastle

BLUEGRASS DISTILLERS ($)

Bluegrass Distillers LLC
www.bluegrassdistillers.com
501 W 6th St #165,
Lexington, KY 40508
Brand: Bluegrass Distillers

BOURBON 30 SPIRITS (N/A)

Bourbon 30 Spirits LLC
www.itsbourbon30.com/gift_shop.html
130 S Water St,
Georgetown, KY 40324

HARTFIELD & CO DISTILLERY (FREE)

Buchanan Griggs Inc.
www.hartfieldandcompany.com
320 Pleasant St,
Paris, KY 40361
Brand: Hartfield & Co

Louisville

EVAN WILLIAMS BOURBON EXPERIENCE ($$)

Heaven Hill Distilleries Inc.
www.evanwilliams.com
528 W Main St,
Louisville, KY 40202
Brand: Evan Williams

JIM BEAM URBAN STILLHOUSE ($)

Beam Suntory
www.jimbeam.com
404 S 4th St,
Louisville, KY 40202
Brands: Baker's, Basil Hayden, Booker's,
Jim Beam, Knob Creek

North

BAKER-BIRD WINERY ($$$$)

River Horse Inc.
www.bakerbirdwinerydistillery.com
4465 Augusta Chatham Rd.
Augusta, KY 41002
Brand: Historic B. Bird

OLD POGUE DISTILLERY (FREE)

The Old Pogue Distillery LLC
www.oldpogue.com
715 Germantown Rd,
Maysville, KY 41056
Brands: Old Maysville Club, Old Pogue

SECOND SIGHT SPIRITS (N/A)

Second Sight Spirits LLC
www.secondsightspirits.com
301 Elm St,
Ludlow, KY 41016
Brand: Oak Eye

West

BARD DISTILLERY (N/A)

Bard Distillery
www.thebarddistillery.com
5080 State Road 175 South
Graham, KY 42344
Brand: Cinder & Smoke

DUELING GROUNDS DISTILLERY ($)

Dueling Grounds Distillery LLC
www.duelinggroundsdistillery.com
208 Franklin Bypass
Franklin, KY 42134
Brand: Linkumpinch

O.Z. TYLER DISTILLERY ($$)

TerrePURE Kentucky Distillers Inc.
www.oztylerdistillery.com
10 Distillery Rd,
Owensboro, KY 42301
Brand: Mellow Corn, Ezra Brooks

R.H. RESOLUTE DISTILLERY (N/A)

Jamieson's Distillery Inc.
3855 Kentucky Hwy 125,
Hickman, KY 42050
Brand: N/A

TYLER WOOD WHITE WHISKEY (N/A)

Tyler Wood White Whiskey LLC
www.whitewhiskey.com
103 White Whiskey Ln,
Lewisburg, KY 42256
Brand: White Whiskey

Appendix: Brand Index

This list was correct as of 2020. Brands are bought and sold, so while comprehensive this list may not always be 100% correct if brands are traded between companies. If it is important that you visit a particular distillery to potentially purchase a specific product, it may be worth contacting them ahead of time or double checking on their website that they still offer the product. You can find a current online copy of this brand index at **www.whiskey-lore.com/brands**.

BRAND	DISTILLERY
Ancient Age	Buffalo Trace
Angel's Envy	Angel's Envy
Baker's	Jim Beam
Bardstown "Fusion" Series #1	Bardstown Bourbon Company
Barrel House	Barrel House
Barton 1792	Barton 1792
Basil Hayden	Jim Beam
Benchmark	Buffalo Trace
Bernheim	Heaven Hill
Bird Dog	Bardstown Bourbon Company
Blade and Bow	Stitzel-Weller
Blanton's	Buffalo Trace
Blood Oath	Lux Row
Bluegrass	Bluegrass Distillers
Booker's	Jim Beam
Boone County	Boone County
Buffalo Trace	Buffalo Trace
Bulleit	Bulleit
Cabin Still	Heaven Hill
Casey Jones	Casey Jones
Chicken Cock	Bardstown Bourbon Co
Cinder & Smoke	Bard Distillery

BRAND	DISTILLERY
Cowboy Little Barrel	Preservation
David Nicholson	Lux Row
Eagle Rare	Buffalo Trace
E. H. Taylor	Buffalo Trace
Elijah Craig	Heaven Hill
Evan Williams	Heaven Hill
Ezra Brooks	Lux Row
Fighting Cock	Heaven Hill
Four Roses	Four Roses
George T. Stagg	Buffalo Trace
Hancock's President Reserve	Buffalo Trace
Hartfield & Co	Hartfield & Co
Heaven Hill	Heaven Hill
Henry Clay	James E. Pepper
Henry McKenna	Heaven Hill
High West	Bardstown Bourbon Co
Historic B. Bird	Baker-Bird Winery
I. W. Harper	Stitzel-Weller
James E. Pepper 1776	James E. Pepper
Jefferson's	Kentucky Artisan
Jeptha Creed	Jeptha Creed
Jim Beam	Jim Beam
John E. Fitzgerald Larceny	Heaven Hill
Johnny Drum	Willett
J. T. S. Brown	Heaven Hill
J. W. Dant	Heaven Hill
Kentucky Amber	Boundary Oak
Kentucky Gentleman	Barton 1792
Kentucky Owl	Kentucky Owl
Kentucky Tavern	Barton 1792

BRAND	DISTILLERY
Kentucky Vintage	Willett
Knob Creek	Jim Beam
Legent	Jim Beam
Limestone Branch	Limestone Branch
Linkumpinch	Dueling Grounds
Longbranch	Wild Turkey
Maker's Mark	Maker's Mark
M. B. Roland	M. B. Roland
Mellow Corn	Heaven Hill
Minor Case	Limestone Branch
Michter's	Michter's
Neeley Family	Neeley Family
New Riff	New Riff
Noah's Mill	Willett
Oak Eye	Second Sight Spirits
OCD #5	Glenns Creek
Old Bardstown	Willett
Old Charter	Buffalo Trace
Old Crow	Jim Beam
Old Fitzgerald	Heaven Hill
Old Forester	Old Forester
Old Grand-Dad	Jim Beam
Old Heaven Hill	Heaven Hill
Old Maysville Club	Old Pogue
Old Oscar Pepper	James E. Pepper
Old Overholt	Jim Beam
Old Pogue	Old Pogue
Old Rip Van Winkle	Buffalo Trace
Pappy Van Winkle	Buffalo Trace
Parker's	Heaven Hill

BRAND	DISTILLERY
Pearse Lyons Reserve	Town Branch
Peerless	Kentucky Peerless
Pikesville	Heaven Hill
Rabbit Hole	Rabbit Hole
Rebel Yell	Lux Row
Rittenhouse Rye	Heaven Hill
Rockcastle	Barrel House
Rock Hill Farms	Buffalo Trace
Rowan's Creek	Willett
Russell's Reserve	Wild Turkey
Ryskey	Glenns Creek
Sazerac Rye	Buffalo Trace
Six Mile Creek	Six Mile Creek
Stave+Barrel	Glenns Creek
Three Boys	Three Boys Farm
Town Branch	Town Branch
Very Old Barton	Barton 1792
Very Old St. Nick	Preservation
Wattie Boone & Sons	Preservation
Whiskey Row	Kentucky Artisan
Whiskey Thief	Three Boys Farm
Wilderness Trail	Wilderness Trail
Wild Turkey	Wild Turkey
Wild Turkey Rare Breed	Wild Turkey
Willett Pot Still	Willett
W. L. Weller	Buffalo Trace
Woodford Reserve	Woodford Reserve
Yellowstone	Limestone Branch

Acknowledgements

THANKS TO:

Chandler Bolt for showing me there is no better time to share your knowledge than now; Scott Allan for keeping my feet to the fire; Matt Emmorey for the nuggets of wisdom as I moved into the publishing phase, and the Mastermind Community and instructors at Self-Publishing Books for providing great advice and critiques along the way.

Emma Gibbs for the yeoman's job you did in brushing up my text, removing inconsistencies, and providing helpful suggestions along the way. Working with you was a pleasure.

To Clint Carter for always being open to my opinion on design, for reading my mind and always coming up with stellar designs, and amazing advice. Thanks for rescuing the reputation of this project.

All of the amazing friends and followers who support me on Facebook, Instagram, and YouTube.

The tour guides, brand ambassadors and owners from each of the distilleries I visited throughout Kentucky. Your love and passion for your product is inspiring. Thank you for sharing your love of stories, history, and amazing spirits.

Cheers!
Drew Hannush

Bibliography

BOOKS

- Crowgey, Henry G. *Kentucky Bourbon The Early Years of Whiskeymaking*, The University Press of Kentucky 2008
- Gardyne, Tom Bruce. *Scotch Whisky The Essential Guide for Single Malt Lovers*, 2019 Carlton Books Limited 2019
- Huckelbridge, Dane. *Bourbon A History of the American Spirit*, HarperCollins Publishers 2014
- Minnick, Fred. *Bourbon The Rise, Fall, and Rebirth of an American Whiskey*, Quarto Publishing Group USA Inc. 2016
- *The Register of the Kentucky State Historical Society, Volume 1.* Kentucky State Historical Society. 1903 pp. 34

CORPORATE WEBSITES AND TOUR GUIDES

- Angel's Envy Distillery
- Bardstown Bourbon Company
- Barton 1792 Distillery
- Boone County Distillery
- Buffalo Trace Distillery
- Bulleit Distilling Company
- Casey Jones Distillery
- Castle & Key Distillery
- Four Roses Distillery
- Glenns Creek Distillery
- Heaven Hill Bourbon Heritage Center
- James E. Pepper Distillery
- Jeptha Creed Distillery
- Jim Beam American Stillhouse
- Kentucky Artisan Distillery
- Kentucky Distillers' Association
- Kentucky Peerless Distillery
- Limestone Branch Distillery
- Lux Row Distillery
- Maker's Mark Distillery
- MB Roland Distillery
- Michter's Fort Nelson Distillery
- Neeley Family Distillery
- New Riff Distillery
- Old Forester Distillery
- Preservation Distillery
- Rabbit Hole Distillery
- Stitzel-Weller Distillery
- Town Branch Distillery
- Wilderness Trail Distillery
- Wild Turkey Distillery
- Willett Distillery
- Woodford Reserve Distillery

INTERVIEWS

- Young, Al. *Personal Interview*. 5 November 2020

SPECIFIC WEBSITE ARTICLES

- Baxter, Debora Ann. "Charles Burks of Washington County" Geni. MyHeritage Ltd. 24 May 2018., *www.geni.com/people/Charles-Burks-of-Washington-County/6000000005961820618* Accessed 20 April 2020
- Drake, Bernie. "When Peoria Tried to Monopolize Whiskey" Peoria Magazine. Central Illinois Business Publishers, Inc. February 2016 *www.peoriamagazines.com/ibi/2016/feb/when-peoria-tried-monopolize-whiskey* Accessed 20 April 2020
- McGrew, Jane Lang. "History of Alcohol Prohibition" Schaffer Library of Drug Policy. *www.druglibrary.org/schaffer/library/studies/nc/nc2a.htm* Accessed 20 April 2020
- "Code of Federal Regulations: Title 27: Alcohol, Tobacco Products and Firearms Part 5: Labeling and Advertising of Distilled Spirits" Electronic Code of Federal Regulations. *www.ecfr.gov* Accessed 20 April 2020
- "Oldest Operating Bourbon Distillery" Guinness Book of World Records. Guinness Book of World Records Limited. *www.guinnessworldrecords.com/world-records/oldest-operating-bourbon-distillery* Accessed 20 April 2020
- *Prohibition: A Film by Ken Burns & Lynn Novick*. Written by Geoffrey C. Ward. Directed by Ken Burns and Lynn Novick, narrated by Peter Coyote, Florentine Films, 2011.

GENERAL WEBSITES

Google Maps/Google Earth

There Is More For You

DISCOVER MORE ABOUT BOURBON AND WHISKEYS AROUND THE WORLD IN 3 EASY STEPS

Join the Whiskey Lore Society and get exclusive interviews and content, discounts, access to a growing list of distilleries, and alerts about upcoming events.

Get travel and whiskey inspiration daily.
Be a part of the conversation at *www.facebook.com/whiskeylore* and *www.instagram.com/whiskeylore*

Learn about bourbon and whiskey history, myths, and legends by subscribing to the *Whiskey Lore Podcast* on your favorite podcast app.

START TODAY

Say "YES" to joining the Whiskey Lore Society:
www.whiskey-lore.com/signup/

Make sure to use the promo code "**bourbon1792**" to get FREE access to the online distillery guide, wish list feature, brand-to-distillery index and to sign up for the *Whiskey Lore Society Newsletter*.

Can You Do Me A Favor?

THANK YOU FOR READING MY BOOK!

I really appreciate all of your feedback,
and I love hearing what you have to say.

I need your input to make the next version of this book
and to help others find this helpful information.

Please leave me an honest review on Amazon
letting me know what you thought of the book.

Thanks so much!

Drew Hannush

READY FOR A KENTUCKY BOURBON ADVENTURE?

Whiskey Lore's Travel Guide to Experiencing Kentucky Bourbon is packed with everything you need to easily plan and prepare an incredible bourbon journey through the Bluegrass State.

LEARN. Find out what bourbon is, understand its history, and learn how it's made, so you can spend your tour time finding out what makes each distillery unique.

PLAN. Whether you choose a tour company or do-it-yourself, I'll help you figure out transportation, accommodations, logistics, timing, how to map out the best distilleries, and how to handle the day of your tour.

TASTE. Handle bourbon tasting like a pro. I'll help you get in the right mindset and prepare your palate so you get the most out of your tasting experiences.

TOUR. You will have all of the practical information necessary to plan a perfect mix of distilleries that fit your tastes and interests.

EACH DISTILLERY PROFILE INCLUDES:

- My top three reasons to visit
- A list of brands produced there
- Elements of the standard tour
- What to expect from the tour, tastings and keepsakes
- Side trips so you can see more of Kentucky
- Planning features like tour times, prices, parking information, and more
- Things to listen for or watch for on your tour
- Additional distilleries within a short drive

ABOUT DREW HANNUSH

Drew is an author, entrepreneur, whiskey enthusiast, and fellow traveler. As host of the *Whiskey Lore Podcast*, he reveals the stories, myths, and legends built around whiskey. Through his social media and travels he helps whiskey lovers develop a deeper understanding of the origins and characteristics of their favorite spirits.

Drew is an avid traveler who has been to all 50 states and visited 75+ distilleries on two continents.

Also included is a distillery-to-brand cross-reference guide and online resources to further enhance your planning experience.

Are you ready for some bourbon travel? Let's go.